When Horses Pulled the Plow

WISCONSIN LAND AND LIFE

ARNOLD ALANEN
Series Editor

When Horses Pulled the Plow

Life of a Wisconsin Farm Boy,
1910–1929

Olaf F. Larson

The University of Wisconsin Press

The University of Wisconsin Press
1930 Monroe Street, 3rd Floor
Madison, Wisconsin 53711-2059
uwpress.wisc.edu

3 Henrietta Street
London WCE 8LU, England
eurospanbookstore.com

Printed in the United States of America

Library of Congress Cataloging-in-Publication Data
Larson, Olaf F.
When horses pulled the plow: life of a Wisconsin farm boy,
1910–1929 / Olaf F. Larson.
p.   cm.—(Wisconsin land and life)
Includes bibliographical references.
ISBN 978-0-299-28204-2 (pbk.: alk. paper)
ISBN 978-0-299-28203-5 (e-book)
1. Larson, Olaf F.—Childhood and youth. 2. Farmers—Wisconsin—Edgerton—Biography.
3. Tobacco farmers—Wisconsin—Edgerton—Biography.   4. Farm life—Wisconsin—
Edgerton—History—20th century.   5. Tobacco farms—Wisconsin—Edgerton—History—
20th century.   6. Edgerton (Wis.)—Rural conditions—20th century.   I. Title.   II. Series:
Wisconsin land and life.
S417.L34A3   2011
630.9775′8—dc22
[B]
2010041463

Contents

Contents

Illustrations

Foreword

JERRY APPS

Olaf Larson is a generation older than I am. He grew up in the early 1900s; I grew up in the 1930s and '40s. We were both farm boys, he in southern Wisconsin, I in central Wisconsin. Although some twenty-five years separate us, we had nearly the same farm experiences. We both grew up driving horses. Neither us had electricity, indoor plumbing, or central heat in our farm homes. And we both grew up during times of great change in farming. To understand these changes, we need to look at some history.

After years of French trading, exploration, and missionary work in what became Wisconsin, the first wave of landowners arrived from upstate New York and New England, beginning in the 1830s (lead miners had arrived in southwestern Wisconsin about a decade earlier). Thousands of German, Norwegian, Irish, Polish, and other European immigrants followed the Yankees, as they were called. Immigrants began arriving in Wisconsin shortly after territory status in 1836 with numbers increasing after statehood in 1848 and continuing into the early twentieth century. By 1900 some fifty different ethnic groups had found new homes in Wisconsin; Germans were the most numerous, followed by Norwegians, Irish, and Poles.

Olaf Larson's father, Sandberg Larson, immigrated to Wisconsin from Norway. He settled near Edgerton in 1903 and married in 1909.

When Olaf was born in 1910, life on a Wisconsin farm had become a bit easier than that of early settlers. Many changes in agricultural practice and farm family life had taken place in the years from statehood to the early 1900s. During the early years of settlement, farmers grew wheat, thousands of acres, but wheat growing had faded into the background and dairy farming had taken over in the southern two-thirds of the state by the time Larson was born. Much of the vast timberland in the northern one-third of the state had been cut, the logs moved off to sawmills. A few pioneers tried farming in the cut-over, but the growing season was short, much of the land poor, and before a crop could be planted enormous stumps had to be cleared. In the southern counties, especially in counties such as Rock where Larson's story takes place, dairying flourished by 1910. It was in that year that Wisconsin for the first time surpassed New York State as the nation's leading producer of cheese.

When Wisconsin moved from wheat growing to dairy farming, farmers built the great barns, many of them still found around the countryside today. Larson describes the barn on his home farm in considerable detail, indicating that the beams and posts came from trees growing on the farm. "The beams showed the marks of the axes that had shaped them from logs," he writes. Larson also recalled seeing reminders of earlier life on his farm—he found an ox yoke and cradle (a special scythe for cutting grain) stored in their barn.

From the settlement years to the years beyond the Civil War, when wheat was king and dairy farming was unknown, farmers planted wheat by hand, harvested it with a hand-operated cradle, and threshed it with a flail—a hickory pole to which a smaller piece of wood was attached with a piece of leather. Sometimes oxen walked over the grain to thresh it. The earliest barns, those that preceded the big dairy barns, were called three-bay threshing barns and were used as a place to thresh grain and to store it. The center of the barn had two large doors, one on each side of the floor where the wheat was threshed. The doors were opened when flailing took place, to allow the draft to blow away the chaff. These early barns did not house livestock. Once dairy began replacing wheat growing, farmers sometimes jacked up the earlier three-bay threshing barns and constructed a basement under them to house cows. The upper part of the barn was used for hay storage. Just before 1900, gambrel-roofed barns began appearing. The cattle continued to be housed in the basement area of the barn; but the upper part, with a gambrel-roof, provided more space to store hay than the simple gable-roofed barns that preceded them.

During the early 1900s, University of Wisconsin researchers began studies to determine effective ventilation systems for barns. Conducting much of this research, Franklin H. King developed what became known as the King Aerotor (a galvanized steel ventilator for dairy barns). King is also credited with developing the first successful round (cylindrical) silo in 1891. Many silos were originally square or rectangular, with much silage spoiling in the corners. The King silo, or Wisconsin silo as it was sometimes called, revolutionized silo building in Wisconsin and throughout the nation.

In the early 1800s, oxen pulled the plows and carts and, in addition to doing the heavy work on the farm, provided slow but steady transportation. Essentially no draft horses of the type that Larson describes on his home farm could be found anywhere in the United States until the 1830s. Draft horses, Percherons and Belgians mostly, but also Clydesdales, Suffolks, and Shires, were imported from Europe. They soon began replacing oxen on farms in many parts of the country. Draft horses were big, weighing up to a ton or more each, much larger than the riding and carriage horses that might weigh only half as much. And a draft horse, especially a team of them, could do the work of a yoke of oxen and much more quickly. Oxen were slow and plodding. It's said that if you drove a team of oxen to church for Sunday services and you wanted to arrive on time, you needed to start out on Friday.

Draft horses arrived on the farm (and in the villages and cities, too) at the same time that many other changes began occurring in rural America. Various farmer-blacksmith inventors began creating new kinds of farm machinery that could be pulled by these newly arrived draft horses. Cyrus McCormick, one of the most noted of these inventors, was a farmer and blacksmith who grew up in Virginia and patented a reaper in 1834. The reaper, pulled by a team of horses, cut grain and thus replaced the cradle, an implement that required back-breaking hand labor. It was a revolutionary invention by any measure, but because a reaper cost considerably more than the inexpensive cradle, many farmers were still cradling their grain in the antebellum years. When thousands of men went off to the Civil War, reapers became more popular.

John Deere, a blacksmith from Vermont, arrived in Grand Detour, Illinois, in 1836. Deere shoed horses, fixed wagon wheels, and quickly learned that the plows the settlers brought with them from the East did not work well in the heavier, midwestern soils. The cast-iron plow's moldboard, which turned the soil, would not scour—that is, soil would stick to it. Deere invented a plow with a shiny steel moldboard, which farmers in the area discovered worked well. His plow was not the first of its kind but soon it became the most successful. John Deere, the company still in business under that same name, went on to develop many other horse-drawn implements designed to make life easier for the farmer.

Many other inventions followed: manure spreaders, grain drills, spike-tooth harrows, disks, corn planters, hay mowers, hay rakes, hay loaders, stationary hay presses, cultivators, and threshing machines— all pulled or powered by draft horses. Truly, a revolution in agriculture was taking place. Modifications and improvements were constantly made to these inventions. For instance, the reaper, which cut but did not bind grain into bundles, was replaced by the grain binder, thanks to an invention by John Francis Appleby, a Civil War veteran who moved to Wisconsin from New York in 1845 and settled near Mazomanie. His device tied a knot in twine wrapped around a bundle cut by a reaper. Now, with a knotter mechanism in place, a reaper became a binder and saved farmers one more bit of hand labor: the binder not only cut the grain and formed it into bundles, but wrapped a string around each bundle and tied it with a sturdy knot.

At the same time that inventors were working on new ways to plant and harvest grain, others were devising new ways to improve upon the flail-and-oxen method of threshing. J. I. Case, another New Yorker, came to Rochester, Wisconsin, in Racine County in 1842 and immediately began manufacturing a threshing machine he had been perfecting back in New York. His machine (early ones were powered with horses) separated the grain from the chaff all in one operation. Case soon moved his operations to Racine where, in 1847, he built a three-story brick manufacturing plant. By the 1860s, the Case threshing machine had become one of the most popular makes on the market.

Early threshing machines had been powered by horses that were hitched to a device called a sweep. Through a system of gears and rods, horse power was turned into machine power. By 1876, the first steam traction machines began appearing. Steam powered and fueled with wood or coal, these ponderous cast-iron beasts became the forerunners of the modern farm tractors (today's tractors use gasoline or diesel fuel).

By the time Olaf Larson was growing up in Rock County, Wisconsin, all of these no longer new inventions had become an important part of farming. Horses continued to do much of the work; the lighter weight tractors, especially those with rubber tires, were still years in the future.

Although farm work in the early 1900s required somewhat less physical labor, especially when compared to farm work fifty years earlier, home life had changed little for hundreds of years. By the middle 1800s, kerosene lamps and lanterns had replaced candles, and woodstoves replaced fireplaces for cooking. But such conveniences as electricity, indoor plumbing, and central heating were still years away. In 1893, at the Chicago World's Fair, Thomas Edison and George Westinghouse demonstrated electric lights, among other inventions, but it would be many years before electricity made its way to the country, and especially to the farms. In 1930, 90 percent of urban homes in the United States had electricity, but only 10 percent of U.S. farms had electrical power. For many farmers, it wasn't until Franklin D. Roosevelt signed legislation creating the Rural Electrification Administration (REA) in 1935 that electric power slowly began making its way onto farms. However, many farmers had to wait until after World War II for electrification.

Olaf Larson's experience was typical of many farm children. A windmill pumped water from the well, a woodstove heated the house, his mother cooked on a wood-burning cookstove, and an outhouse stood a discreet distance from the house. A cistern located under the kitchen captured rainwater from the roof. A cistern pump attached to the kitchen sink provided cistern water—mostly for hand washing as it was often contaminated with leaves and other debris.

Larson describes a farmstead typical for a farm of that day. The cluster of buildings resembled a tiny village. The barn was usually the largest and most important structure, especially once dairy farming became the predominant agricultural pursuit. Farmers repaired and improved their barns long before they did the same for their homes. They said, "The farmhouse is where we live, but it is the barn that provides our living." Other buildings included a granary, corncrib, chicken house, brooder house (for young chicks), a hog house, machine shed, pump house, sometimes a smokehouse, and, in Olaf Larson's case, a tobacco shed for storing their cash crop, tobacco.

The farmhouse, usually the second largest building in the farmstead, was the center of farm operations. The big farm kitchen, with wood-burning cookstove, had a large kitchen table with a kerosene lamp in the center. There the family ate and read newspapers and magazines, children did homework, mother worked on her knitting or clothing repair, and neighbors were entertained when they stopped by for a visit. A pantry off the kitchen provided a storage place for groceries and dishes; in the cellar under the house were stored canned fruits and vegetables, plus potatoes, onions, and other vegetables.

In addition to the cookstove in the kitchen, most farm homes of Olaf Larson's era had a second woodstove in the dining room. The stove pipe offered a meager amount of heat as it passed through the upstairs bedroom to the chimney. Many farmers closed off the other rooms of the house during the winter and did not heat them. Most farm homes had parlors (living rooms) where the family could entertain relatives; stage special occasions, such as weddings; and, when a death occurred in the family, display a casket.

One can think of farm communities as being in concentric circles. The farm family and the farmstead made up one circle. Mother and father and several children provided the work force and worked as a team. Father took care of the farm animals, managed the growing and harvesting of crops, and generally supervised the entire farm operation. Besides cooking, doing laundry, cleaning the house, and tending to bumps and scrapes, the farm wife usually managed a large vegetable garden (with help from the children) and was responsible for the chicken flock. Money from the sale of eggs went to buy groceries and birthday and Christmas presents.

Each child had chores, assigned according to age. Carrying in wood from the woodpile to the house became a task for a three- or four-year-old. As the child got older, chores included carrying in water from the well, feeding chickens and hogs, gathering eggs, hauling in straw to bed the cows, throwing down silage from the silo, milking cows, hoeing the garden, and eventually hauling manure and helping with field work, which meant driving horses. Everyone was expected to do chores without being reminded and without complaint. If a child was ill, a sibling would double up on chores. Farm children learned how to work at an early age, to the best of their abilities, and they expected neither praise nor payment for their efforts. Working together went along with being a part of a farm family.

The one-room country school district made up the second, larger circle of a farm community. All the students in the district walked to the country school, usually not more than two miles, so the school district was about four miles square. The country school, besides providing education for grades one through eight (with but one teacher), gave rural communities an identity. Ask a farmer where he was from and he would usually recite the name of the country school his kids attended. The country school also served as the social center of the community. It was here that the community celebrated birthday and anniversaries and attended the Christmas program to see the neighborhood kids perform, An annual highlight was the end-of-the-year picnic, where everyone feasted on a potluck lunch and the students played their fathers in softball. In many places, the country church also helped bring the community together through Sunday services and such activities as ice cream socials, summer picnics, and fall festivals.

Threshing and other work bees, in addition to providing a way for farmers to harvest their grain with neighbors' help, offered yet another social outlet for farmers. Storytelling and practical jokes, plus enormous meals provided by the host farmer's wife, were all part of the threshing bee experience.

In addition to helping each other to thresh, stock wood piles, and fill silos, neighbors stood ready to help each other in times of need—serious injury, a fire, a tornado ripping apart a barn, illness. With outside assistance often miles away, neighbors depended on each other.

The third circle, beyond the farm family and the school district, was the nearby town, which offered what the family could not provide on the home place. It included a grocery store, a post office, a meat market, a church or two, clothing store, lumberyard, hardware store, grist mill, a drugstore, a harness shop, a couple of saloons or more, a restaurant and hotel, a livery stable (until autos came along), a cheese factory, and train depot. The village cheese factory bought the farmer's milk, and the grocery store traded groceries for his wife's eggs. During the warm months, Saturday night was "town night." In winter it was Saturday afternoon. Country villages usually had small populations and were located no more than eight or ten miles apart so horse and buggy could easily manage the trip, though seldom more than once a week.

Farm life followed a seasonal cycle, from the earliest history of farming. These seasonal patterns were sharply defined in the North, where the winters were harsh, the snow piled deep, and no field work could take place. Olaf Larson describes this cycle well: "When the snows melted and the frozen ground thawed and the robins returned from the South, we knew spring was at hand."

While winter on a dairy farm involved milking cows twice a day, cleaning the barn, keeping the animals fed and comfortable, in spring a flurry of new activity took place as farmers spread manure, plowed fields, and planted crops. Farmers were up before dawn and fell exhausted into their beds not long after sunset as the relentless challenge of caring for crops and then harvesting and storing them took place, day after long summer day. Most farmers did not work on Sundays, although the cows still had to be milked morning and evening. There was little time for recreation; no farmer ever took a vacation. It was not until the last cob of corn was shoveled into the corncrib in November that farm work slowed down a bit in preparation for winter and less stressful times.

Farmers then and now depended on the weather: enough rain for their crops, but not too much; warm temperatures, but not too warm. Farm kids looked forward to rainy days, for these were days of rest. A chance to crawl up in the haymow of the barn and listen to the drum of raindrops on the roof, rest, and nap.

The predictable seasonal cycles on the farms were sometimes interrupted by forces over which the farmer had no control, especially the weather but also national recessions, depressions, and wars. Olaf Larson recalls the effects of World War I. His father had to register for the draft in 1917, and his uncle Paul was called to serve. Many store-bought items became unavailable, such as syrup (the Larson family grew sorghum cane and made their own). Olaf and his school-mates saved nut shells, which were used in making gas masks for soldiers. Students were encouraged to buy war savings stamps for twenty-five cents each. Wars also usually meant higher prices for farm products.

With the end of the war in 1918 came a decline in farm prices that continued to the Great Depression, which began in 1929 and didn't end until 1941, with this nation's entry in World War II. With these wild swings in farm prices, farmers often diversified. Rather than depend solely on one income source, such as milk sales (in Wisconsin), they also raised hogs, sometimes sheep, and almost always chickens. Most farmers during the early and middle 1900s also grew cash crops, such as tobacco, potatoes, green beans, and cucumbers. Generally, farm families were able to survive quite well because they always had something to eat, had a roof over their heads, and were never out of work. Farmers with large mortgages on their farms fared less well during hard times, and many lost their farms.

New inventions and new technology influenced farming practices during Olaf Larson's boyhood on the farm, just as they do today. He recalls that when the first tractor came into the neighborhood, about 1919, the teacher walked the students down the road to watch this new piece of quipment at work. In 1926 the Larsons got their first car, a Ford Model T.

Before and during World War II, many farmers operated as they had during Larson's time—they farmed with horses, managed with kerosene lamps and lanterns, and had few conveniences in their homes. All of this changed and changed dramatically in the postwar years. Soon farmers had electricity and telephones, owned tractors, bought combines to replace threshing machines, purchased milking machines and increased their herd size, began using hybrid seeds, and drove pickup trucks. Farmers bought out their neighbors and farms got larger; young people left the farm in droves to find work in the cities.

Country schools closed, threshing bees disappeared, and farm communities were transformed. Changes continue to this day. In enormous so-called factory farms, thousands of cows are milked in one location, with none of the animals ever spending a day outside on pasture. Hogs and chickens are raised under similar conditions. New technology, much of it computer based, continues to influence and alter how farming is done.

Olaf Larson gives us an insightful look into agriculture and farming in the early twentieth century, along with family life on the farm. We are indebted to him for his effort, for to understand what is happening in agriculture today, we must appreciate what it has been.

Preface

When my sons were growing up, they liked to hear my stories about growing up on a Wisconsin farm. Some stories they asked for over and over. To my surprise, my grandchildren also liked to hear some of the same stories. In time, I came to realize that a more complete account in writing might be of interest to my family. But one professional writing commitment after another kept me from getting to the task. Finally, at age ninety-eight, I have found the time to prepare this account.

Looking back, I realize how close in time I was to the early settlers of that part of Wisconsin. It was not more than seventy years before I was born that the farm was first occupied and the clearing of the forests started for farmland. The original house, a log cabin, of the original owner of the farm still stood close to the house in which I was born. Artifacts in the barn were reminders of the agricultural technology available to the original occupants. The ox yoke was a reminder that oxen, not horses, were used when the land was first plowed. The cradle was a reminder of the hard labor required to harvest grain before the invention of the horse-drawn grain binder. The scythe was a reminder that hay was cut by hand before the horse-drawn mowing machine.

Looking back, I also realize that I grew up when inventions, new ways of doing things, were appearing. We got our first automobile in 1926; before that we went by horse-drawn vehicle—buggy, wagon, cutter, bobsled. The first tractor in the area was a curiosity. Listening to the radio was something new. Few farms had electricity; we did not. The sound and sight of an airplane was so unusual that we would stop work in the field to watch.

Daily life was local. The country schools were located so that every child would be within walking distance. Most social contacts were local. We did not shop or go visiting any farther than it was convenient to go by horse and buggy and return home the same day.

We did not have much cash income, but we lived well. We had ample production of good food for family use. We had our own supply of firewood to heat the house. The water supply brought up from deep in the ground by a windmill was of excellent quality. We were also a part of the market economy. Most of the livestock products were sold with the farmer having virtually no control over price.

Looking back, I have come to understand that the adults I grew up with on the farm had important values, explicitly stated or implicit. They included hard work, independence, self-reliance, honesty, frugality, care of the soil, care of the livestock, avoidance of debt, and doing no harm to others.

I thank the two anonymous reviewers of the manuscript for their careful reading of it and for their questions and helpful suggestions. I also thank Gwen Walker, acquisitions editor at the University of Wisconsin Press, for her assistance.

I am indebted to my granddaughter Jacqueline Claire Larson for taking my handwritten, sometimes illegible draft and rendering it into a readable manuscript.

I thank her mother, Debra Larson, for taking time from her busy schedule to prepare the final copy.

I submitted this work for publication because of the repeated urging of my son Richard and the interest expressed by other family members and a diverse set of individuals outside the family.

When Horses Pulled the Plow

1

The Setting

Family, Farm, and Locality

Olaf Fredrick Larson, was born February 26, 1910, at my parents' home on a farm in Fulton Township (Section 27), Rock County, Wisconsin. I lived on that farm until the fall of 1928, when I left to attend the College of Agriculture, University of Wisconsin, in Madison. I returned to the farm to work for my father during the summer of 1929. Visits home were fairly frequent over the next five years, when I was at the university. But I was not again involved in the day-to-day farm operations until my father was killed in a farm accident in June 1943. I then returned to operate the farm until the fall of 1944.

Family

I was the only child born to Sandberg and Clara Alwin Larson. My father was born on the island of Vega, south of the Arctic Circle, off the coast of Norway, when Norway was not yet independent of Sweden. He was the third of six children, the second son of Ole and

Marie Larsen (the spelling was changed by immigration officials to "Larson"). The family lived on a farm purchased by their ancestors in 1855. The farm was called Grottland and is identified by that name (and variations) in records going back to 1541. The farm provided a residence and subsistence. The main source of livelihood was fishing at sea.

After completing elementary school, my father went to sea as a fisherman. In early 1903, a serious illness at sea led to his decision to come to the United States. On September 9, 1903, at the age of twenty, he sailed from Trondheim to Hull, England, then to Quebec, Canada, and from there by train to Edgerton, Wisconsin. He said he arrived with one five-dollar bill in his pocket, speaking little, if any, English. He carried with him a certification as to his good character from the police officer of Vega and a certification that he had completed *Folkeskol* (elementary school). He soon found a job as a hired man on the John Hurd farm, probably the largest farm in the area. A photo taken with the Hurd family shows him working with a large flock of sheep.

I developed early an awareness of my Norwegian "roots." My father corresponded some with his father, and I knew when his father's letters came and were read. My grandfather wrote to me (in Norwegian) and sent me postcards with scenes of Vega. My father's younger sister, Theresa, came to the United States in 1911, her first stop being with my parents. She soon married a Norwegian and lived in South Milwaukee. The contact with her through visits, when she and my father spoke Norwegian, further reinforced my awareness of my Norwegian ties.

My father and me

I recall that in 1914, when I was four, my father received his naturalization papers. When he came home after the proceedings, I knew that he was excited and proud to now be an American citizen.

My mother was born in Rock County, where she lived all of her life, to Christhof and Ernestine Alwin. The Alwins emigrated from Germany about 1883 or 1884 and became tenants on an 80-acre farm, where my mother was born. She was one of six children, four boys and two girls. Her father died at about the age of forty, apparently from diphtheria. The widowed mother continued to operate the farm, with the help of the family, until she married a widower with a 195-acre farm.

At the age of twelve, my mother was put out to work as a hired girl on a farm between Milton and Edgerton. It is uncertain whether she finished elementary school. Later she became a hired girl for the John Hurd family farm, where my father was a hired man. She early developed an interest in recordkeeping. In 1905, at age eighteen, she started to keep a detailed account of her expenditures—the date of purchase, the item, the cost. She continued this for almost a year after her marriage. She was the one who kept our farm records.

When I was quite young, I developed an aversion to identification with anything German. I was only four when World War I started, eight when it ended. But I was old enough to hear adults talk about the atrocities of the German "Huns," about "Kaiser Bill," about reported German plans to poison public water supplies. I heard about pro-Germans being tarred and feathered, about barns of pro-German farmers being painted yellow. My mother knew some German, because of her parents, and one time I was teased at school because my mother could speak German.

My parents were married on March 29, 1909. The first year after marriage, they grew tobacco in a share arrangement on the Charles Adolphson farm of 400 acres a few miles from Edgerton. When I was a child, I recall going, by horse and buggy, to visit the Adolphson family as well as the Hurds. Before I was born, they moved to the Grant Walrath farm as tenants on a share basis.

The Farm I Grew Up On

There is no evidence that there was a written lease with Grant Walrath. Rather, the arrangement was by an informal verbal understanding. My father provided the labor (including any he hired), the farm equipment, the horses for draft power, and half the cattle and other livestock. Grant Walrath provided the land and the farm buildings and house, maintained the buildings and fences, and provided half the livestock. Income from the farm was divided equally.

At the time, the Walrath farm was operated with 160 acres; of this, the Walraths owned 120 acres and rented for cash 40 acres from Grant Walrath's sister who lived in Milwaukee. She had inherited the land when their father's estate was settled. After Grant Walrath died, in 1922, the rental was discontinued. Of the remaining 120 acres, about 75 acres was tillable cropland, and the rest was used for pasture and woods.

The nature of the land on this and surrounding farms was shaped by the last Wisconsin glacier. It was at the southern edge of the glacier that left level and rolling areas, suitable for crops, and hills filled with gravel or sand, suitable only for pasture or trees. Most of the cropland on our farm was a silt loam, but one field was on the sandy side. One of the fields used only for pasture and woods had two small depressions usually filled with water, which served the livestock on pasture and also attracted waterfowl. Sometimes, when rains had made it deep enough, one of the ponds was my swimming hole.

As I grew old enough to help with the farm work, I came to know every foot of the tillable land by plowing it, fitting it for planting with disk and drag, and cultivating it. Likewise, I came to know every part of the pastured and untillable land, walking over it when getting the cows from pasture, hunting for rabbits and woodchucks with my dog, riding over it on my pony, looking for spring flowers and gooseberries, and picking nuts. One feature that always intrigued me was the massive gully washed out years past in a slope of sandy soil. The upper part of this gully had been covered with a layer of cement to minimize further erosion. At the lower edge of this cemented area there was usually a hole dug by a woodchuck and sometimes occupied by skunks.

Settlement of the Area

Settlement by white man of this part of southern Wisconsin began in the 1830s. This was long before passage of the Homestead Act of 1862, so settlers purchased the land from the federal government at $1.25 per acre. Much of this land was covered by trees, especially burr oak, although there were clearings within the forest. First to arrive in what was my neighborhood were the two Stone brothers and another man who in 1836 bought land along Rock River. In the 1840s what became our farm was acquired by Grant Walrath's father, Jacob, who came from Pennsylvania with his brother, Sylvester, who bought an adjoining 160 acres. Shortly after getting their land, both brothers joined the California gold rush, then returned to clear the land and build their farms. What became the county seat for Rock County, Janesville, some ten miles from our farm, was settled in 1835. Edgerton, which was our main trading center, was settled in 1853. (Wisconsin had become a state in 1848.) The first passenger train came to Edgerton in 1854. *The Edgerton Story*, a history of Edgerton prepared for its centennial in 1953, recounts that one of the first passenger trains got stuck in a snowdrift about one mile from the depot and was pulled to the depot by four yoke of oxen. A bridge was built so the train could get over Rock River. If the engineer blew the locomotive whistle as the train approached this bridge the sound carried, so I remember hearing it when outside on our farm several miles away.

Indian Predecessors

Sac and Winnebago Indians had occupied this area before white settlement. They had villages or camps close to the Rock River not too far from where I grew up. The river started from Lake Koshkonong, a shallow lake with marshy surroundings, which was a great area for fish and waterfowl. I grew up with reminders of this Indian past. About two miles from my country school was the small hamlet of Indianford, whose name reflects its convenience as a place to cross the river. When I was in the eighth grade, I was on a school picnic at Indianford when, with a small group of other students, we decided to explore the path on a ridge above Rock River. We soon came upon an Indian burial ground, desecrated with human bones lying on top of the burial mound.

One day when I was quite young, I explored the second floor of the log cabin close by our house. The cabin had been the original house on our farm. There I found a basket partly filled with a variety of Indian arrowheads, differing in size, color—because of the rock from which they were made—and quality. There were also spearheads and scrapers. When I grew older and did work in the fields, I was on the lookout for arrowheads. I found only one, of poor quality, which I spotted as I walked across a field.

The Other Side of the House

Grant Walrath had given up operating the farm because of severe asthma caused by the dust and pollen. But he and Mrs. Walrath wanted to continue to live on the farm so they added rooms to the original house. One side was used by the Walraths and Mrs. Walrath's father, John Porter, who was a native of England. The other side was used by my family. The door between the two sides was never locked. The Walraths had no children. As a child, I had the run of both sides of the house. So I grew up in an atypical situation, one that gave me experiences and opportunities I would not otherwise have had. When I was a small child, I would sometimes find out what the Walraths were to have for their meal. If it was more appealing to me than what my mother was preparing, I would say, "Guess who's going to eat at your house?" That usually got me the desired invitation.

The Walraths gave me a red metal wagon, which I used a lot. When I was about ten, Mr. Walrath bought me a white Scotch Collie puppy, about six weeks old, which I named Jack. The Walraths would sometimes pick me up at my country school and take me to a church supper at a hamlet called Fulton. They also took me with them to visit their friends who were vacationing in the summer on a lake.

Mrs. Walrath entertained a lot. Guests included a doctor and his family from Janesville, the owner of a tobacco warehouse and his family from Janesville, a farmer from near Janesville who bought cattle to feed for market, and a building contractor from Edgerton with several children, the oldest my age. I met these people, and my family was sometimes included at the meals.

Mrs. Walrath liked books and music. In her living room were glass-fronted bookcases with perhaps three hundred books, all fiction. When I was old enough, I was free to read any of them. My introduction to music came from listening to recordings, played first on a table model Victrola with a horn and then an upright Victrola in a beautiful wood cabinet. Occasionally, both families would listen to recordings for an evening.

Grant Walrath continued some tasks on the farm, such as caring for several hives of honeybees. Located near the fruit orchard, the hives were a source of honey. In the spring he set up the supers, the upper story of the hives where the bees stored the honey they collected. Later in the season, he would take the honeycombs from the supers. The two families used the honey. He also liked to fish and had a supply of metal fishing rods and a variety of reels. One time he, my father, our hired man, and I took a wagon drawn by a team of horses to a large pond on a farm I had never been to before. There the men waded into the water with a long net with which they caught quantities of pike. They put the fish in a wooden barrel, took the fish-filled barrel home, and placed the fish in the large water tank used by the livestock. These fish provided quite a few meals.

Mr. Walrath probably had more education than most farmers in the area. I recall his mentioning attending Albion Academy, which was located three miles north of Edgerton. He had two part-time jobs. One was the elected assessor for the Town of Fulton. As assessor, each year for tax purposes he had to place a value on all the taxable property in the township. The other job was buyer for a tobacco warehouse owner in Janesville, M. F. Green and Sons. On a seasonal basis he went to "northern" Wisconsin—I heard Viroqua and La Crosse mentioned—to buy tobacco directly from farmers. On his return from one trip he brought, for my father, a fine set of harnesses. I had never seen so much brass fittings on a harness for a workhorse. Mr. Walrath's employer provided him with a car. The first was an Oakland coupe, the second was a Paige coupe. He was used to driving horses and had never before had a car. On the day he brought the first car home, he started to back it up to where it was to be stored for the night. But he forgot how to stop it and was heard shouting "whoa, whoa" until the car stopped when it ran into the side of a barn.

One consequence of living in the same house as the Walraths was the relationship I developed as a young boy with Mrs. Walrath's father, whom I called Porter. I never knew my grandfathers; one was in Norway, the other was dead. Porter, in retrospect, became a surrogate grandfather. When I was five or six, he took me on my first fishing expedition, down the road to the large pond on the neighboring farm. Porter was a master gardener and I learned something about gardening from him. His specialty was onions, each properly spaced, grown in long rows, always weed free. He would put a burlap bag filled with fresh horse manure in water in a wooden barrel. In a few

Grant Walrath, owner of the farm my father rented, with my dog, Jack

days, the liquid provided fertilizer for the onions. In one corner of the garden, he built a trellis and planted grapes, and in the fall clusters of blue and white grapes hung from the trellised vines. On warm summer evenings he would sit under an elm tree in a high-backed chair, smoking his pipe. If I came by to sit with him, he would tell stories about his past experiences. On one occasion, after Grant Walrath died, a large swarm of bees settled in the crotch of the elm tree by the front gate to our house. Porter put on overalls, tied tight at the bottom, put mosquito netting over his head and face, donned gloves, and put an empty beehive on a white piece of cloth. Then he climbed a ladder to where the bees were. Soon he came down the ladder, covered with bees. He had the queen, put her in the hive, and all the bees followed.

Grant Walrath died in middle age when infection set in following an appendix operation. At the meal in our kitchen following the funeral, Mrs. Walrath asked my father if he would continue as a tenant. In the years that followed, she became very dependent on my parents. She did not drive horses or cars. When my parents went to town to shop or to social events, she generally went with them. As her health deteriorated, she and Porter often ate their noon or evening meal in our kitchen.

Our Neighborhood and Beyond

The neighborhood, for me, corresponded with the boundaries of our country school district, Cox District No. 2. What made this a neighborhood was the school, mutual aid (work exchange) among farmers, and some social activities. The brick, one-room schoolhouse was at a crossroads. The sixteen farms in the district, each with one family except for ours, which had two families, were in four directions from the school. Our farm, a mile from the school, was at one end of the district. Between our place and the school were five other farms. In the other direction were eight farms, the furthest about one and a half miles from school. On the other crossroad, there was one farm in each direction.

Eleven of the sixteen farms were owner operated and five were tenant operated, but one of these was more like an owner because the land was owned by the operator's father, who lived on the adjoining farm. Three of the tenant farms were owned by the same absentee owner. These were "family-size" farms ranging from 80 acres to a little over 200, with one possible exception. The largest farm I knew of in the area was the one where my parents had worked; it had 651 acres in 1919, according to the *Prairie Farmer's Reliable Directory of Farmers and Breeders, Rock County, Wisconsin.* Three of the farms usually had a hired man year-round; some of the others had one hired man by the month during the busy season. Some hired a man by the day as needed.

There was a mix of nationality backgrounds—German, Norwegian, Danish, Canadian, along with the "old-line" Americans of British background. This was not a church-going neighborhood; I knew of only one couple who attended church regularly.

EDGERTON

The place we went to most often for groceries and other goods and services was Edgerton, about five miles away. In 1910, with a population of 2,513, Edgerton had barely crossed the 2,500 U.S. Census line from "rural" to "urban." It continued to be a small place while I was growing up, with a population of 2,688 in 1920 and 2,906 in 1930.

Edgerton was the center of what rural sociologists might call our "trade center" community. The stores were mostly on one side of the main street, Fulton Street, with a few services on one of the three side streets. The streets were lined with hitching posts to which we tied the horses for the buggy or the team for the wagon or bobsled we rode into town. A drinking fountain for the horses could be found on the main street.

All the stores were locally owned and family operated. One store sold only groceries. A second had a grocery area but also sold dry goods, such as "yard goods" to make clothing. A third had a two-story department store along with the groceries. And a fourth, run by an elderly couple, carried some groceries in the back part of what was a "variety" store. The last had a candy counter in front of the store where licorice sticks or candy could be bought for a penny. This was a great attraction for me when I was younger. In the grocery departments, in all stores, the customer told the clerk what was wanted and the clerk would bring the items, weighing and packaging any item kept in bulk form, then assembling the purchases on the counter in front of the customer. Customers paid by cash or check, no credit cards. For some, such as my mother, payment might be covered in part or full by the eggs brought in. The largest store had a fleet of horse-drawn wagons to deliver groceries to the families in town who called in their orders by phone. This store-customer relation began to change in the 1920s when an A&P store appeared in Edgerton, the first outside corporate business in this field.

There were two stores for men's and boys' clothing. The one my father and I used most was a well-stocked, well-established store owned by two partners. It was they who usually waited on us when we bought overalls, work shirts, footwear, and other items. On the rare occasion when a suit was bought, it was customary to ask that a belt or pair of suspenders be "thrown in." The request was always granted. The relationship with this store was such that when I was in high school and I needed a small amount of cash, I would write a check, sign my father's name, and be given the money. The other store bought pelts of trapped animals, such as skunks. I got a dollar or more for a skunk skin; the less the white, the more I received. At one time this store installed a platform-like device. When you stood on it, it lit up and you could see your feet in your shoes, supposedly a way to ensure a good fit when buying.

Another store of importance to me was the bakery. When we were in high school, my friends and I sometimes went to the bakery to treat ourselves to a cream puff for a nickel. There was also a candy counter with penny candy. If you got a pink center instead of a white one, you got a free piece. Other stores on the main street included the partner-run butcher shop with sawdust on the floor and wood chopping blocks for cutting meat. In the back of the market hung carcasses of beef and other animals. One time they came to our farm and bought a cow, which they butchered right there. At the proper season of the year one would see wooden barrels filled with lutefisk, each piece standing upright like a board. These barrels most likely came from Norway.

There was a hardware store, two drugstores with soda fountains (I liked to treat myself to a chocolate milk shake, costing fifteen cents, when in town on a summer Saturday night), and a book and music store run by two brothers. This store was the only place to buy schoolbooks. On a side street were two furniture stores. The owners of each were also undertakers.

The two locally owned banks were close to each other. My family used both. When I was quite young I started a savings account at the Tobacco Exchange Bank. By the time I started college I had accumulated five hundred dollars, from earnings, gifts, and the sale of orphaned lambs I had raised.

On one of the side streets was the blacksmith shop where my father had his horses shod and plowshares sharpened. The smithy usually worked with the door open. I was always intrigued with the smell, the sound of hammer on anvil, the light of the fire that heated the horseshoes to red as they were shaped. I liked to see the smithy's skill in handling large workhorses as he put on the shoes.

At opposite ends of the main street, across from the stores, were two farm implement dealers. One was John Deere, the other—which my father used—was International Harvester. Here my father bought new farm equipment when needed and, every year, a supply of binder twine. The twine was used in the grain binder to bind sheaves of grain as it was cut and in the corn binder to bind corn into bundles as the stalks were cut. I liked to go to the International Harvester place to look at the new machinery and, in my younger years, the buggies that were in stock. This dealership was run by two rather hefty brothers who had a small office. Sometimes my father would stop in the office to talk. If I was with him, I would sit and listen to the talk. The brothers employed a man who was good at repairing machinery. If there was a repair problem my father could not handle, this man would come to our farm to do the work.

Before Prohibition, Edgerton had saloons, five, I believe. They were well patronized, especially on Saturday nights, and only by men. After Prohibition, a couple of the saloons were converted into pool halls. These, in the view of the high school superintendent, were off-limits to high school students on school days. If the superintendent got word that a student was in a pool hall, he soon appeared to take corrective action.

Edgerton, like most places its size and larger, had a livery stable. It was on the main street, perhaps a block or so away from where the stores ended. Here, farmers could leave their horse or team if the weather was bad or if they were going to be in town so long they didn't want to leave their horses tied to the hitching post on the street. The stable also had horses and carriages for rent for salesmen and others who might need transportation to get around the area. At this time it was not uncommon for families living in town to have a horse with a small barn alongside or in back of the house and, in some cases, a carriage house. When I was in high school, there were three automobile dealerships—Ford, Chevrolet, and Buick.

Services included two lumberyards and two feed mills. Every week or two my father would put oats, barley, or corn in bags in the wagon to take to one of the mills to be made into grist to feed the cattle and hogs. The other feed mill was at the Edgerton Farmers Warehouse, which sold feed, seed, and farm supplies.

Other services I recall included a laundry, a shoe repair shop, a tailor—whose son was a school classmate—and barbers. There were several doctors, dentists, and lawyers. The veterinarian who came to our farm to test our cattle for tuberculosis and Bang's disease lived in Edgerton. There was a movie theater, admission twenty-five cents. Generally, there was a newsreel, a short comedy, one part of a serial, and the feature picture. These were the days of silent movies with the conversation showing in print on the screen. Music to accompany the feature film was provided by a piano at the front of the theater.

On Saturday nights, when the weather was warm, on the corner by one of the banks, one could always find a highly decorated popcorn wagon, dispensing a bag of hot buttered popcorn or a bag of peanuts for a nickel. This popcorn wagon was pulled to its location by a horse.

On the same street was a stone- or brick-fronted hotel, with a restaurant, which became a bus stop when the Greyhound bus started to come through Edgerton.

The park, away from the center of town, had a bandstand where concerts were played on summer evenings. I recall attending them on a few Wednesday evenings with the Walraths or my parents. At the edge of the town was a fairgrounds with grandstand and horse racetrack, neither of which I saw used. The fairgrounds did, however, provide the space where the high school football team practiced and played its games.

Important in giving the community identification was the high school I attended. Although not a consolidated or central school, it drew students from the surrounding countryside. Directly in back of the high school was the public library, which I used frequently from the time I started high school. The library always had the distinctive odor of the product used to keep the floor clean. In high school my three best friends were farm boys who lived in the direction opposite from Edgerton from where I lived. On Saturday nights, when we knew we were going to town with our parents, this was our meeting place.

The station for the Chicago, Milwaukee and St. Paul Railroad was about a block from the main street stores. The railroad had both passenger and freight services. My friends and I liked to go to the station and watch the passenger trains, with their steam locomotives, come in. The station operator was also the agent for Western Union, sending and receiving telegrams. The train brought the mail for Edgerton's post office. There it was sorted and then, for families in the surrounding countryside, delivered six days a week by Rural Free Delivery.

The hub of the telephone system for the area was the switchboard with its operators. In the country there were numerous "party line" arrangements, each serving a few families who could call each other directly. But to reach a family on another party line, one had to go through the central switchboard operator. So, too, long distance calls were placed through the operator.

Churches were Catholic, Congregational, Methodist, and two Lutheran, one for Germans and the other for Norwegians. I never saw the inside of any of these except for the Congregational. When I was in high school, its minister started a Boy Scout troop, which my parents permitted me to join. My membership was short lived but I did get to go to scout camp for two or three days. There I was shocked when I saw the minister smoking a pipe. At that time I did not think that was appropriate behavior for a minister. I had one unforgettable experience with respect to the Catholic church, which was located next to the high school. One night when I came out of the school, after a club meeting, a cross was burning in front of the Catholic church. I never heard this talked or written about. However, a few years earlier there was Ku Klux Klan activity in the Janesville area. When it was started, my father went to one meeting, perhaps out of curiosity. When he came home, he told about men wearing hoods and sheets and about burning crosses.

There were three cemeteries close to each other, one for Catholics, one for Lutherans, and one for everyone else. On the way to and from town, we had to pass by these cemeteries, two on one side of the road and one on the other. It was always a bit frightening to me when we had to pass these cemeteries at night.

An imposing Masonic temple stood on the main street on the same side as the stores. Opposite the Masonic temple was the police station, staffed by only one full-time officer, as I recall, and a jail with a few cells. Nearby was the firehouse for the equipment used by the volunteer fire department.

Also at one end of the main street was a building for a maker of patent medicines. The most important manufacturer was the highway trailer plant, started at the time of World War I. A creamery, operated by one man, was located in a part of town with poorer houses. Until we started selling whole milk, the cream from our farm went to this creamery, where it was made into butter.

Edgerton was known as the Tobacco City. Its weekly newspaper, locally owned, was the *Wisconsin Tobacco Reporter*. Commercial tobacco growing started in 1854 on a farm not far from town and became an important cash crop for farmers. This led to the first tobacco warehouse being built in 1869; by the early 1900s there were as many as fifty-two warehouses, most of them controlled by outside tobacco companies. The warehouses were mostly in rows on the side of town opposite the main street, south of the railroad tracks. The large buildings were of a yellowish brick, which came from the clay in the pits nearby. Tobacco came to the warehouse from the growers in bundles of thirty or thirty-five pounds, wrapped in a special heavy paper called tobacco paper. Known as "leaf" tobacco, it was used not for cigarettes but for such products as cigars, pipe smoking, and chewing. Before being made into these products, the stem had to be removed from each leaf. "Stemming" was a hand operation, performed by women in the winter months. At that time, a tobacco odor permeated the air.

Edgerton's population was all white with the exception of one family. The man of this family was a barber whose daughters had graduated from high school long before my day. In high school I knew a brother and sister from a Jewish family. There were a few Seventh Day Adventists from the Albion area three miles north of Edgerton. One of them became one of my best friends. One was a star football player. I was never aware of the distinction between Catholic and Protestant or among the Protestant denominations when I was in school.

INDIANFORD

Next to Edgerton the place most visited was Indianford, about three miles from our farm and through which we drove on every trip to Edgerton. It consisted of a hamlet on both sides of a dam, which provided electric power, and a bridge over Rock River. The fishing was good there, with the structures at either end of the dam offering an especially good location for fishermen. When I was young, Porter took me to Indianford. When I was older, I would ride my pony there for a fishing outing.

An unpainted, ramshackle-looking building stood above the river-bank. In it lived an older couple, he a woodworker. Near the entrance was a counter from which she sold a few items, such as bread and candy. On the opposite side of the road, closer to the bridge, was a small store that catered to fishermen. Along with groceries it sold bait and rented boats. Across the bridge was another store, occupied at some times, not at others. When an elderly couple sold their store in Edgerton and moved here, this was the one my mother used if she ran short on something and didn't want to go to Edgerton. Once when she got home after making some purchases, she found that she had been undercharged six or seven cents. She immediately sent me on my pony to pay what we owed to the storekeeper; this was a lesson in honesty I learned from my mother. The kindly storekeeper rewarded me with a piece of candy.

The town hall for the Town of Fulton, a white-painted, one-room building, was also located in Indianford. The building served not only for town meetings and a polling place on election day but also for social events, such as dances and parties. I recall going there with my parents in winter, when the team of horses hitched outside was covered with blankets to keep them warm. The town hall was also used to conduct meetings, which must have been sponsored by the extension service whose county office was in Janesville. It was at one such meeting that I heard a civic leader from Janesville talk about 4-H clubs. That led to my becoming a club member for four years, raising a calf each year, which I took to show at the county fair in Janesville.

Indianford had an elementary school and a small building close to one end of the bridge, ownership unknown to me, which seemed to be seldom used. At one time, Sunday school classes were started there, sponsored, I think, by the Congregational church in Fulton. Some adults urged me to go, so I rode my pony to attend. I found that the principal teacher was a young woman whose intellect was not highly regarded by my family. I thought there was more emphasis on collecting money than I liked. My Sunday school attendance ended after going two or three times.

The other thing at Indianford that made a lasting impression on me was the icehouse. This was an underground storage area covered over by a roof. In the winter, when the water on Rock River was frozen to a sufficient thickness, men would saw the ice into large blocks, haul them to the icehouse, and pack them in sawdust. (In those days we didn't have refrigerators.) There the ice lasted well into the summer. If we wanted to make ice cream we went to the icehouse, bought a block of ice, took it home, broke it into small pieces, and packed the ice cream freezer with ice and rock salt. Then we hand-turned a paddle inside the freezer long enough to produce our homemade ice cream.

OTHER DESTINATIONS

The only other place where we did any trading was Janesville, about ten miles from our farm Before we had a car, going to Janesville was an all-day event.

Upon arriving, we left our horse at a livery stable for a fee of about twenty-five cents. We ate the lunch my mother had packed at a place, provided as a community service, where families from the country could eat, use the restroom, and rest a bit. The trip usually included a stop at a big department store, which I considered the fanciest store I had ever been in, with nicely dressed sales ladies and an unusual system for handling money. When the salesperson received the money, she put it and the bill in a small container that was sent at a high speed on a set of overhead cables to a cashier. In a few moments, the container with the change and receipt came speeding back to the salesperson. After we had a car, in 1926, we went to Janesville on Saturday nights to sell the eggs and buy groceries at a store that paid more for eggs and sold groceries for less than did the Edgerton stores.

The county fair was held in late summer in Janesville. The family almost always went for a day to see the livestock and exhibits and to buy tickets to sit in the grandstand to watch the harness races (horses pulling a two-wheeled sulky) and the performance on the platform facing the grandstand.

I did get to go to a few other places. We visited my maternal grandmother in Milton, about seven miles away. Sometimes the Alwin family got together at her house for Thanksgiving dinner. Milton had a Fourth of July celebration with events for children, such as bag races and three-legged races, tug of war for men, and an afternoon baseball game. I always liked it when I got to go. On the way to Milton, we passed the farm where my mother first worked as a hired girl; she always pointed this out to me.

Madison, the state capital, was about thirty-five miles away. I was quite excited when I got my first view of the capitol building. My father had taken me with him to a farm to buy a ram, and the farmer pointed out the dome in the far distance. The only time I got to Madison before I was a high school senior was when my uncle took my mother and me to see the zoo.

The most distant place I went was South Milwaukee, where my father's sister lived with her family. We tried to go there about once a year. At first, we went by train to Milwaukee and then by streetcar to South Milwaukee. When we got a car, we drove the seventy-five miles. The first time we went, we ran out of gas and my father had to go to a farm to get gas. The Ford Model T had no gas gauge.

Beyond My Locality, 1910–29

Certain events and activities during 1910–29 affected my life at that time, which I recall years later. Among these was World War I. When the war started in Europe in 1914, I was four years old, too young to read but aware of the newspaper headlines. Entry of the United States into the war in 1917 brought it close to home. My father had to register for service and talked about the possibility of going. I went to a going-away party for my Uncle Paul, who was being called into the army, but the war ended before he had to go.

We could not get some things, such as white flour, at the grocery stores. My mother did not like to have to use the barley flour, so we got white flour by taking wheat we had grown to a mill especially designed to grind wheat into flour. One time, my father took me on the all-day trip with team and wagon—taking the wheat and coming back with sacks of flour and bran, the by-product. As a substitute for syrup, we planted sorghum cane. At harvest time, we cut the stalks, pulled off the leaves, cut off heads that had seed, and took the stalks to a farmer whose cider press could squeeze the juice out of the canes. My mother boiled down the liquid to make a dark, not-very-good-tasting sorghum to put on pancakes and use in baking.

People were called on to support the war effort in various ways. One way was to save nut shells, which were used in making gas masks for soldiers. In our country school, the teacher sold us war savings stamps for twenty-five cents each. We pasted them in a book, which, when filled, could be redeemed for a war bond. One school project was the making of gun swabs used by soldiers to clean their guns. We took white material, such as sheeting, cut it into one-inch squares, and made strings of one hundred squares.

Everyone wanted the war to end. On a Sunday visit in the summer of 1918 with my parents to a farm family, after the noon meal, I went with the men to a barley field where we looked for the letter *B* on the leaves. The *B* was supposed to mean "the boys will be in Berlin before Christmas." Perhaps my most vivid memory of World War I is the day in November 1918 when a farmer who had just come from Edgerton stopped by our school to tell us that the war was over. School was immediately dismissed. I jumped on my pony to go home, thinking of the time of Paul Revere and his ride to let the colonists know that the British were coming. As I galloped past each house on the way home, I shouted, "The war is over! The war is over!" It turned out that this news was a day too early.

The war brought good prices and "good times" for farmers as a whole. An indication, in our case, was when (it must have been spring 1918), on a Sunday in our living room after dinner, my father offered my uncle seventy-five dollars a month to work for him. No one present had heard of such a high wage for a hired man. But soon an agricultural depression set in, lasting through the 1920s and merging into the Great Depression, which started in 1929. One response by Congress to solve the "farm problem" was legislation to have the U.S. Department of Agriculture encourage farmers to organize purchasing and marketing cooperatives. In Wisconsin there was a big effort to get tobacco growers to form a cooperative to market their tobacco—a controversial issue among farmers in our area. My father did not join.

A farmers' organization called the Nonpartisan League in the Dakotas became a quite influential force on behalf of farmers. It sent organizers into Wisconsin to get members. My father was persuaded to sign up and pay the dues. The only tangible result of this that I could see was receiving the organization's periodical, *The Nonpartisan League.* My father's membership was short term.

Other events on the national scene that impacted our area included the flu epidemic of 1918, the passing of the constitutional amendment in 1918 giving women the right to vote, and the Volstead Act, which prohibited alcoholic beverages nationally. Giving women the right to vote did not create much stir in our family or community. It was said that women would vote like the men. But Prohibition was another matter. On the Saturday night before Prohibition was to go into effect, the Edgerton saloons did a thriving business. Prohibition was the topic of the day, the men calling out to each other, "Near beer! Near beer!" (which was to be the legal substitute for the real thing) as they passed each other on the street. In a short time, speak-easies, which sold alcoholic beverages illegally, appeared. Men seemed to have no trouble finding out where they were. In social gatherings, I often heard the adults talk about making home brew or wine. My family did not do either. But in the fall one or more of the big wooden barrels of cider made from apples in our orchard was allowed to become "hard," helped on by the addition of raisins to the cider. A bootlegging business developed, apparently centered in Chicago. On some Saturday nights, one or more fancy, large cars were parked on the main street. Word got around that these belonged to bootleggers reported to have a hangout of some type on Lake Koshkonong, not far from Edgerton.

During 1910–29, the United States had five presidents, starting with Republican William Howard Taft. He was followed by Democrat Woodrow Wilson (1912–20), the World War I president, and Republicans Warren Harding, Calvin Coolidge, and Herbert Hoover. Word of Harding's death in office was brought by a neighbor who had been to town, on a day when the grain threshers were at our place.

Taft's predecessor was Theodore (Teddy) Roosevelt, who headed a third-party ticket in 1912. My father seemed to admire Roosevelt. In Wisconsin, Robert (Fighting Bob) La Follette was a prominent and controversial political figure. He had been governor of the state and U.S. senator who launched an unsuccessful third party in 1920 to seek the presidency.

Except for the anti–La Follette talk, I do not recall hearing much talk by the Walraths and other adults about the candidates at the time of any presidential campaign. It was local politics that brought on discussion. It seems that each time there was an election to decide who would chair the town board, the governing body for the Town of Fulton, there was a contest. Time after time, a faction led by a farmer of German background, with a large extended family, sought the office. My folks were opposed.

2

The Farmstead and Farmhouse

The farm was on both sides of the country road that passed by it. On one side was the barn and forty acres. On the opposite side was the house with the eighty owned acres and, in the early years, the forty rented acres. On the barn side were two fields separated by a lane and about twenty-five acres of pasture and woodland. The lane went from the barnyard to the pasture and woodland.

The house side had about fifteen acres of pasture with some trees. The orchard and lawn space around the house occupied perhaps two acres. The owned cropland was divided into four fields; the most remote part of these was a half mile from the house. A lane ran between two fields to reach the area used mostly for pasture.

Most of the fences along the road and along the line separating our farm from adjoining farms were woven wire, barbed wire, or a combination of the two. But still in use was rod after rod of the wooden rail fences built decades earlier. Two sides of one pasture-woodland had a total of about 120 rods of such fence. A second such area had 40 rods of rail fence on one side. Two other stretches of fence were rail. These rail fences were made from logs split into

12- or 14-foot lengths. The way the rails were laid resulted in a zigzag pattern. These fences, about 5 feet high, were strong enough to not be broken through by horses, cattle, or sheep. I learned how to maintain these rail fences by putting back rails that had been knocked off and seeing that each zig and zag was properly braced by a short piece of rail.

These grayish, weathered rail fences were not only, in my view, an attractive feature of the landscape but good for wildlife—birds, rabbits, and other creatures. Grass and weeds could grow tall, and wild berries grew in the spots inaccessible by plow or cultivator because of the zigzag pattern.

The Barn and Other Farm Buildings

The barn was built parallel to the road about twenty feet from its edge. The barn had two levels. The framework for the upper level was made of massive beams and posts, which came from the trees growing on the farm when it was purchased. The beams showed the marks of the axes that had shaped them from logs. The whole framework was held together by ingenious use of mortises and joints, all held together by wooden pegs. Not a nail, bolt, or other piece of metal could be found in this framework. The framework was covered by wood boards running vertically. The nails that attached each board to the framework were unlike any commonly used today: square at the head and below. The upper level was set on a foundation of quarried stone and could be accessed from ground level because the barn was built on a slope.

The upper level was more interesting and made the barn unique as compared with the other barns I knew in the neighborhood. Two large doors in the center of the barn faced the road so that a wagon-load of hay or bags of grain could be pulled in by a team of horses for unloading. Next to these large doors was a small door to a small, windowless room. Here stood the De Laval cream separator used for separating cream from the whole milk. On one wall hung tools and such items as hoes and scythes. But here also hung a yoke for oxen, a reminder of earlier days when oxen, not horses, pulled the plows. Another reminder of the past was a cradle, the device with a scythe used for cutting grain at harvest time before the horse-pulled reapers (grain binders) were adopted. In back of this was a room for grain storage, if needed. In it was a fanning mill, used every spring before planting time. The grain to be used for planting was put in this device, which had a large fan, cranked by hand, and a set of screens. The fan separated the light kernels, not suitable for planting, from the heavy kernels of grain, which were planted. Off this room were three large grain bins in which the oats and barley, in separate bins, were stored at threshing time.

The drive-in area had haymows on either side, a half-mow over the rooms just described, and a full mow on the other side. The hay was pitched from the wagon to the mows.

Originally the lower level was used mostly for horses. My father's horses were in stalls at one end. Mr. Walrath, initially, had five or six horses for driving, which were together in a box stall. In the center of the barn was a box stall for the bull.

Our barn before the silo was built

All this changed when the barn was remodeled shortly before 1920. The barn was extended. The lower level now had stalls for seven horses, which faced the wall. The main part of this level had two rows of stanchions for the cows, each row facing a wall. In a corner was a bull pen. All of this equipment for the cattle was purchased. At the time of remodeling, a silo made of wood staves was put up, blocking access to the barn's upper level through the two wide doors. In addition, a hay track was installed under the roof of the barn. This setup allowed the hay to be pulled into the barn from the loaded wagon standing outside the barn and dropped into the mow where wanted. The device involved a big "hayfork," which was stuck into the hay on the wagon, then pulled up on a rope attached to the hay track and pulled along the track with a thick, strong rope that went through a pulley out the other end of the barn and was pulled by a horse. The horse was driven at first by either Porter or my mother. Later, when I was old enough, I had to be the driver.

About fifty feet from one end of the barn was a four-part structure that extended along the length of one side of the barnyard. The first part was the cow barn, which we called the "old cow barn" after the cows were moved into the remodeled barn. It had one row of stanchions to keep the cows in place. Each stanchion had two heavy wooden parts, which must have been made on the farm. The cow's head was placed between the two parts, and a U-shaped piece of metal held the parts together. Cows entered the cow barn from the barnyard by a door that was divided horizontally. The upper part could be left open to provide light and air. The only other source of light was a small opening, a wooden sliding panel, at either end of the barn. Overhead, not more than a foot above the head of the tallest of the men, were roughly hewn poles stretched from beam to beam. The poles were spread a few inches apart, not making for safe footing if one went up there for any reason. Hay was stored atop the poles, giving the cows below some protection from the winter cold. The old cow barn was used for calves or for hogs, as needed, or not at all. Sometimes a stray hen would find her way in and we would discover that she had made a nest and laid eggs in it.

In the next part of the structure, one-quarter was penned off for the sheep, and the rest was used for hogs. This part also had poles overhead. When the barn was remodeled, a hay track was also installed under the roof for the cow barn part and the sheep-hog part.

Next came the corncrib. A driveway ran through it so a wagon loaded with ears of corn could be driven in and the corn shoveled, scoop by scoop, into the two storage cribs on either side. These cribs were slatted for ventilation to help dry the moisture from the corn.

The corncrib held a corn sheller with a hand crank. An ear of corn inserted in the sheller passed between two metal cylinders, which removed the kernels from the cob. The kernels dropped into a pail below and the cob came out the other end. The cobs fueled the kitchen stove, and the kernels fed the chickens.

Until cars replaced them, two buggies were kept in the corncrib drive-through. Overhead, two cutters, or sleighs, were stored until winter, when snow made the use of buggies impractical.

Next in this set of buildings was a tobacco shed where tobacco leaves were "cured." It had two drive-throughs for unloading the stalks from the tobacco rack on the wagon. The shed had vertical rather than horizontal siding. Every few feet a board had hinges so it could be opened to provide the ventilation needed to ensure that the tobacco leaves cured properly.

At the corner of this shed was the stripping house where the leaves were stripped from the tobacco stalks, usually between late November and the end of February. It had one room downstairs and one room upstairs.

At right angles to the stripping house was a second tobacco shed similar to the first. The drive-throughs for both sheds were used for storing farm equipment unless it was in almost daily use or was used seasonally for a few days. One of my father's cardinal rules was to not let equipment stand out in the weather, if it could be helped, and get rusty.

At one side of the barnyard, quite close to the barn, was a wooden structure we called the milk house. It contained the large water tank for the cows and horses, inside of which was a little tank that kept cream and milk cool. The water came first to the little tank, through an underground pipe from the well on the other side of the road. In winter, when the large tank could freeze over, a water tank heater was fired up to keep the water ice-free so that the animals could drink.

Just beyond, at the corner of the barnyard, was the henhouse. It was large enough for 100 to 125 laying hens and 10 or 12 roosters. In cold weather, the chickens were confined to the henhouse, but otherwise they could be outside, free range, in daytime.

After Mr. Walrath got his first automobile, he put up a building parallel to the road with room for two cars on the side entered directly from the road and room for farm machinery on the other side.

All the farm buildings were painted red.

The House and Grounds

The white frame house was opposite the barn, on the other side of the road. It was built, I believe, around 1870 except for the three rooms that the Walraths added when they decided to continue to live on the farm after it was rented. As I knew the house, it had twelve rooms, six used by my family and six by the Walraths. On our side, the kitchen was at the back, entered from a small porch. A pantry was off one side of the kitchen, the living room off another side. There was one

Me, in front of the farmhouse

downstairs bedroom. Upstairs, at the head of the stairs, was my small bedroom. A large bedroom with two beds opened off a long hallway. At the end of the hall was a small attic with a low ceiling. In it were a spinning wheel and quilting frame. In the hallway was the trunk my father brought from Norway. It held the greenish suit with white stripes that my father had bought just before leaving Norway. Dried tobacco leaves kept the suit moth free.

The Walraths had a living room, small bedroom, dining room, and kitchen downstairs, and a small bedroom and one large bedroom upstairs. A porch extended all along the front of our side of the house. It had a door that went into our living room and also a door into the Walraths' living room. The Walraths had a small screened-in porch off their dining room. This porch was also at the front of the house.

Under one corner of our kitchen was a cistern that stored rainwater. The water came off part of the roof, into the eaves trough, and down a spout where the water could be diverted into the cistern or to the ground. The cistern water was not for drinking, but for other purposes, such as washing your face and clothes. Leaves sometimes accompanied the rainwater into the cistern, resulting in an unpleasant odor. A pump, beside the metal sink where we washed our hands and face, drew the water from the cistern. A wood-burning cookstove stood at one side of the kitchen. The kitchen was the most-used room in the house. It was a place not only to cook and eat, but also to gather after the day's work was done, to read the paper, play card games, and talk.

The pantry was lined with shelves that held all the dishes and the groceries. Most importantly, this was my mother's workplace for washing dishes and food preparation, such as peeling potatoes and washing vegetables. This was all done on a zinc-topped table-like piece that had a flour bin on one side. A three-burner kerosene stove in the pantry served when it was too hot to use the kitchen stove. A pail with a dipper held our drinking water. On some winter mornings, I would go to the pail for a drink of water and find that I had to break the ice to free the dipper to get my drink. Also stored in the pantry were the shiny metal "shoes" for the tobacco setter (planter), greased and carefully wrapped in a cloth, along with the shears my father used for clipping wool from the sheep. When attached to the setter, the shoes covered the roots of the tobacco plants with soil as they were placed in the ground.

The living room stove generally used wood for fuel, sometimes coal. Sometimes, when soot from this wood-burning stove accumulated in the chimney and stovepipe, we had chimney fires. My father had to get up on the roof, pour salt down the chimney to put out the fire, and later clean the stovepipe and remove the soot from the bottom of the chimney, a dirty job. A wall-to-wall carpet lay over a thin bed of oats straw, which was replaced every year or so with fresh straw. This meant taking out all the tacks that held the carpet down at the edges.

My mother kept her sewing machine in the living room, and there was a couch for taking naps. Otherwise, the living room was generally used only when we had company. Off the living room was a small closet. A heavy-gauge, unloaded shotgun always stood just inside the door of this closet. The shells were kept on a high shelf in the pantry.

In the bedrooms, what we think of as mattresses made use of materials from the farm. Inside one cover of heavy cotton ticking were feathers—probably goose feathers. Another mattress had oats straw and a third had dry cornhusks.

The original house was over a cellar. The thick walls were of quarried stone; no water ever came through. The walls must have been eight feet high. The cellar was always cool in summer, and I never knew things to freeze in winter. In one corner of the cellar, beside the stairway to our pantry, was a good-sized room called the milk room. It had whitewashed walls and shelves for the jars of canned fruits and vegetables. It also had a specially made piece of equipment on which containers of milk and cream, as well as other items, such as eggs, could be placed to be kept cool and not invaded by mice.

In the other part of the cellar was a potato bin where freshly dug potatoes were placed each fall. Usually the supply lasted until the next year's crop was ready. Other harvested vegetables, such as carrots and beets, were stored along the wall in sand, which kept them usable through much of the winter. Ears of seed corn for next year's crop were stored in two structures, with wood slats on the sides and bottom, suspended from the ceiling.

Close by the house was the original dwelling, a well-preserved log house that had one room at the lower level and one upstairs. The fireplace had been removed. The floor was dirt. When I was old enough to know about Abraham Lincoln, I wished that I, too, had been born in a log cabin. I imagined how I, like Lincoln, could read and write on a slate in front of the fireplace. Now, the first floor of the log cabin was used to keep piles of split wood for the Walraths' kitchen stove.

The first dwelling on the farm, a log cabin built around 1840 by the first owner

Back of the log cabin, pretty much out of sight, was the out-house. A few yards away was the small brick smokehouse in which hams were smoked by a wood fire that my mother kept burning for days. In summer, the men took their baths in the smokehouse, in the tub of an old washing machine with water brought from the kitchen. Next in this line of buildings was a small, unpainted shed that held a large barrel for kerosene. In the spring, my mother put a broody hen in here to sit on eggs until they hatched. Sometime around 1920, a family from Janesville, friends of the Walraths, decided to give up keeping chickens. Their small chicken house ended up on the same side of the road as our house, and was only used in warm weather.

A tall windmill stood in the front yard, close to the road. It pumped water from a dug well, ninety feet deep, that supplied our water for drinking and cooking purposes. A pipe from the well pump could be directed to the large concrete tank close to the road, from which animals drank when the lane to the pasture ran close to it. I was sad when a pet lamb, almost fully grown, fell into the tank and was found drowned. Or the water could be directed to the pipe that went under the road to the tank on the barn side of the road. Getting the water depended on the wind blowing to turn the fan at the top of the windmill. If the wind did not blow enough for several days, the water for the animals had to be pumped by hand. This was a tedious task. Finally, my father bought a small Fairbanks-Morse gasoline engine to do the pumping in place of wind power. A wooden platform was on the top of the windmill. When the gears attached to the windmill fan became squeaky, my father had to climb a narrow metal ladder attached to the windmill's framework to get on the platform and oil the gears.

A few steps away from the kitchen door, a big, black cast-iron bell was mounted on a post. In years past, the bell was rung to let the men working in the most distant part of the farm know that it was mealtime. The bell no longer worked but the big metal clapper was still there. I liked to push it against the side of the bell to hear the sound. One day my little finger got caught between the clapper and the side of the bell. My finger was cut and I lost the nail. Eventually, the bell was removed.

An orchard of perhaps an acre was a part of the grounds. The orchard had apple, cherry, and plum trees, along with red, white, and black currants and rhubarb. The earliest apple to ripen was the Yellow Transparent, followed by the red Wealthy and the striped Dutchess. Later came the Northern Spy, Plum Cider, and a delicious crab apple. Mr. Walrath planted a large number of trees of other varieties, but when they started to bear, we found that few bore really good eating or cooking apples. The dozen or so red sour cherries were usually productive, as were the plums. When I first knew the orchard, the horseradish that had been planted beneath the trees had gotten out of control. All of it was dug up and carted away.

The beehives were close to the orchard. Nearby, Porter had made a hotbed with a southern exposure. He had dug out the soil beneath and put in large quantities of horse manure before replacing the soil. Tomato and other plants started growing in the hotbed until ready to be transplanted to the garden.

A well-kept lawn was in front of the house and on both sides. Not much grass grew behind the house because the woodpile was there — chunks of wood for the living room stove and split wood for the kitchen stove. Mrs. Walrath had Porter grow a variety of flowers next to the road. At one point, she asked my father to dig up the lawn at one edge and put in a large bed of iris. Several purple lilacs were at the back of the yard. A big, shapely elm stood by the gate, which opened on a well-worn path going to the house. Another large elm stood at one corner of the log house. Smaller elms lined the lane alongside the lawn. Along the road, three large black walnut trees produced an abundance of nuts. When they fell from the trees, they were still covered with the green husk, which turned to a blackish color as it disintegrated. The husk had to be fully removed before the nuts were dried and stored, then cracked during the winter to get the nutmeats used in cooking. At the corner of the grounds, a distance from the walnut trees, was a tall maple tree that Porter sometimes tapped in spring to get sap for maple syrup. This may not have been a sugar maple—its yield was limited. Four trees not native to this area had been planted close to the house years ago. On our side of the house was a cedar, a towering pine with small cones, and a long-needled pine with large cones. Soon after Christmas Day, when I was still preschool age, I saw where a cedar branch had been cut and reluctantly concluded that was where our Christmas tree came from. The tall pine was not far from my bedroom. When the wind blew, I could hear the branches make a sighing sound, sometimes for hours. When the large cones fell to the ground in the fall, they were gathered to fuel the kitchen stove. The fourth tree was in front of the Walraths' porch, close enough to the house to hang a hammock.

At one side of the front gate were two hitching posts where visitors could tie their horses. At the top, each had a metal horse's head with a hitching ring attached. On the other side of the gate, the mailbox was mounted on a post. The box had a red metal flag to raise to alert the mail carrier that the box held a letter for pickup or money to purchase stamps.

3

Crops

Most of our cropland was in field corn (maize); the grains, oats and barley; and hay. The ear corn was used to feed the hogs; some went to the horses along with oats; and some was mixed with oats to be ground for feeding the cattle and hogs. A small part of the crop was shelled for the chickens. A few choice ears were saved as seed for the next year's planting. The leaves and stalks from the bundles of corn cut with the corn binder, after the ears were husked, made fodder for the cattle in winter when they were not in the barn.

After we had a silo, a few acres were used for ensilage. Cut when the stalks were still green but the ears were maturing, the corn was taken to the silo where the ensilage cutter cut the stalks and ears into short pieces and blew them up a pipe and into the silo. Sometimes my father planted sorghum cane, along with the corn, for silage.

After the corn was up, pumpkins were usually planted in a small section of one field closest to the buildings. A few of the ripe pumpkins found their way into my mother's pumpkin pie. When I was old enough, a few became Halloween jack-o-lanterns. But most were loaded onto a wagon, taken to the cow pasture, and broken up for the cows to eat.

Each fall, we selected ears of corn to be used as seed for the next year's crop. When old enough, I liked to take a big bag, walk along the rows of ripe corn, and pick the ears to be saved—good shape, good size, on a sturdy stalk. The seed corn was stored in specially made bins in the cellar.

The oats were mainly to feed the horses, but some was ground for cattle and hogs, some went to the sheep at lambing time, and some to the chickens. It was not unusual to broadcast turnip seeds in a small part of the oat field, after the oats were planted. After the oats were harvested and removed, the field might be used by sheep, who liked the turnips.

Barley is a much heavier grain than oats. It was never fed unground to the hogs or cattle. On rare occasions, some of the barley was sold for brewing beer. In addition to the oats and barley, a few acres of spring wheat were sometimes planted and, less often, a smaller acreage of winter rye. The wheat was used for flour and livestock feed, the growing rye field for hog pasture in the summer.

Every year, a few acres of Evergreen sweet corn, a white-eared corn, were grown. We ate some of the corn, freshly picked and tender. But most was cut when the stalks were still green, loaded on the wagon, and taken to pastures when they were dry from heat and limited rain. The cows quickly ate all of the corn.

Most of the hay was a combination of alsike clover and timothy; part was only timothy. Some years, mammoth clover was grown; its plants were much larger than those of alsike clover. Horses were fed only timothy hay. The rest was for the cattle and sheep. If there was more hay than the barn could hold, it was put into long, high stacks.

My father loading hay with a hay loader attached to a wagon

When the cattle needed hay, a hay knife would be used to cut across the stack to make the hay easier to pitch onto the wagon.

Most fields had a regular rotation of corn, grain, and hay. A year or two of hay was followed by a year of corn, then a year of grain. Then the rotation was repeated.

Five acres of tobacco were planted each year, usually in one of the two fields closest to the farm buildings. The fields were level and the soil well suited for tobacco. Once in a while, parts of two other fields were used. The tobacco fields always received more barnyard manure than the other fields. The check for bundled tobacco delivered at the warehouse was the largest amount of money received at one time during the year. Tobacco was sold by the pound, and the price was set before the crop was delivered. The buyer came to the farm after

Putting a load into the barn's haymow

When the barn was full, we stacked hay in the field

the leaves were bundled, examined them for quality, and made an offer, to be accepted or declined. But one year, when buyers were anxious to ensure the manufacturers had an adequate supply, the buyers bought when the tobacco was still growing in the field. That year, the price per pound was the highest my father had ever been offered. But one day when only a part of the crop had been harvested and was safely in the tobacco shed, there was a bad hailstorm. The hail damaged the leaves of all the tobacco standing in the field. The price for the hail-damaged tobacco was about half that for the undamaged.

We planted enough Irish potatoes to last us from one harvest to the next. And we ate a lot of potatoes—almost always for breakfast, always at noon (our "dinner"), and usually at the evening meal (our "supper"). When the new crop of potatoes was ready to use, all the potatoes left over in the cellar were fed to the hogs.

The garden was some distance from the house, on the barn side of the road, in the corner of a field where the ground was level and fertile. Porter's garden for the Walraths was on the side adjoining a rail fence. In one of the zigzags on the fence, he built a seat where he could rest and sit and look at the garden. Right alongside Porter's was the garden my mother planted and tended. It usually had beans (both green and yellow), beets, cabbage, carrots, cucumbers, dill (for making cucumber pickles), leaf lettuce, onions, parsnips, peas, peppers, radishes, rutabaga, swiss chard, and tomatoes. She also found room at the edge of the garden or elsewhere for Hubbard squash, a large winter squash with vines taking a lot of space. The garden gave an abundance of vegetables, most used fresh the day they were brought to the house. Some of the onions, beets, and carrots were stored in the cellar for winter meals. And some years, cabbage was made into sauerkraut in an earthen crock and kept in a cool place to ferment.

When I was perhaps six or seven years old, I persuaded my mother to let me have a few feet at the end of the garden to plant as I wished. I had read in a farm journal an ad for the R. H. Shumway seed company, so I sent for the catalog and looked for things I might like to order, different from my mother's. One year, I ordered soybeans, rarely grown in Wisconsin at that time. The ripe beans were supposed to make a good substitute for coffee. When I read about hybrid corn, a new development in agriculture, I decided to experiment and used some of my space for a few hills of corn. The first year, I self-pollinated some of the ears, taking the pollen from the tassel at the top of the stalk and putting it on the silk of the ear on the same stalk. Then I covered the ear with a bag to prevent its pollination from a different stalk. The next year, the self-pollinated corn was cross-pollinated with another. The following year, the seeds from the cross-pollinated corn produced some strange-looking, small, misshapen ears. Years later, I learned more about plant breeding when I took an agronomy class in my first year in the College of Agriculture at the University of Wisconsin. There I got one head of Oderbrucker barley, a variety newly developed by a plant breeder in the agronomy department. I planted the kernels from this one head of barley in my garden to demonstrate to my father the virtues of this smooth-awned barley.

Along the garden was a strawberry bed. Every year or two, a new bed was started using young plants from the old bed. We usually had an abundance of freshly picked strawberries, some for jam or sauce. In the corner of the field directly across from the garden, in the sandiest soil of our cropland, we always had a big patch of watermelons and muskmelons. I learned to "thump" watermelons to see if they were ripe. The watermelons grew so large that one was all I could carry to the water tank or cellar to cool. When quite young, I sometimes took my red wagon to the patch so I could bring back more.

To maintain soil fertility we rotated crops, applied animal manure, and plowed under the sod (from the hayfields) and corn stubble. No one had ever heard of "organic" farming at that time, but everything we grew was organically grown with one small exception. If there was a bad infestation of potato beetles, the potatoes were sprayed with Paris Green, a type of pesticide then in use. My father bought commercial fertilizer only at tobacco planting time: five pounds of nitrite of soda, from a drugstore. One tablespoon of nitrite of soda was added to each new barrel of water attached to the tobacco setter. Every time a "click" indicated that a tobacco plant should be placed in the soil, a small quantity of nitrite of soda water left the barrel.

I learned from my father about controlling soil erosion. Two fields had places where the slope was such that the soil was subject to erosion. We tried to keep these places grass covered, and every time we went over them with plow or cultivator, we were to avoid disturbing the grass cover.

4

Livestock

My father never owned a tractor. All of the plowing and other such work was done by horses. Until I was sixteen, my family made every trip to town by horse-drawn buggy or wagon, cutter, or bobsled. *Prairie Farmer's Reliable Directory of Farmers and Breeders, Rock County, Wisconsin*, published in 1919, showed only a short list of tractor owners in Rock County. Only one neighbor was on the list. His was a 10–20 Bull. The day he started using this tractor, our teacher dismissed the school so all the pupils could walk down the road to see this strange new farm machine at work in the field.

Horses

Each of the horses had a name. Pat was the only one raised from a colt. The others were purchased. In his later years, Pat, a big draft horse, became wheezy. Breathing was so difficult for him when he was put to work that eventually he was put to death. Prince, a bay Percheron, was our pride, admired by all horse lovers. He was well built, well mannered, and hard working. Prince was teamed up with Flora, a Clydesdale. Flora was "collar-proud," unwilling to pull her share of the workload, always lagging behind Prince. She was the only one of our horses that ever exasperated my father. Dan and Nancy were a well-matched pair of Belgians. The first driving horse I knew was Barney. When he was sold, he was replaced by high-spirited Dot. She was the one most often hitched to the buggy to go to town. A second driving horse was Princess, a quiet, compact horse who seemed to get less attention than any of the others. At plowing time, it was customary to put the two driving horses, Dot and Princess, on the walking plow that my father sometimes used. Dot was always ahead of Princess.

The horses that were not only used on the farm but driven on the highway were always kept shod. If a shoe was lost or if the shoes no longer fit because their hoofs had grown, the horse was taken to the blacksmith in Edgerton. He cut back the hoof (as one would a long fingernail) and fitted the horse with a new pair of shoes. Shoes were attached with horseshoe nails driven into the hoof. In summer, a fly-net was attached to the harness. In winter, if a horse had to stand in the cold at a hitching post for long, it was covered with a horse blanket.

I do not remember just when I learned how to drive a horse, to put on a horse collar properly, to put on the harness after the required currying and brushing, and to bridle a horse after slipping off the halter, which confined the horse in the stall. But I vividly recall the day, in the summer I was twelve years old and the school term was over, when my father told me I was to start helping with the regular farm work. My task that day was to hitch a team of horses to a riding cultivator, go to a nearby field, and cultivate the corn now a few inches high. I had always gone barefoot in the summertime, but

My father driving four workhorses

one could not be barefoot and control the corn cultivator so the shovels would not uproot the hills of corn. From that day on, I had to wear shoes throughout the year.

Horses were valuable. Prince, for example, cost two hundred dollars. Care was taken to work and care for them properly. After the winter layoff from hard work, the horses were out of condition for the spring work of plowing and other hard field work. They were not worked hard at first. They might get painful muscle strain, making it difficult for them. In hot weather, care was taken to not let the horses get overheated. When cultivating corn, it was customary, in hot weather, to rest briefly after a few rows had been cultivated. One summer, when it was unusually hot, we used five horses instead of the usual three to pull the grain binder.

Cattle

When my father moved to the Walraths' farm, the cattle were grade Durhams. About the time of World War I, three purebred registered Milking Shorthorn cows were purchased. Milking Shorthorns were considered a dual-purpose breed, good for both beef and milk. Shorthorns were popular with Rock County farmers. In 1919, they were second only to Holsteins, a dairy breed known for high milk production. The progeny of our three Shorthorns gradually replaced all the grade cows so that we had all purebred, registered animals. Each calf to be kept was given a name that was registered with the Shorthorn Breeders Association office in Chicago. For a number of years, every heifer was named Strathallan Milker with a number suffix: 1, 2, 3, et cetera. Information on each registered animal was published in a "herd book." Mr. Walrath bought a set of these, updated regularly. When he died, Mrs. Walrath gave the set to me. I spent hours poring over these herd books, which showed the ancestry of every registered animal in diagram form, like a family genealogy.

A new herd sire (bull) was purchased every three years. The best of these was Snowstorm's Duke, all white in color and outstanding in his characteristics. He was selected, with a few other choice Milking Shorthorns in Rock County, to be shown and compete at the international livestock show in Chicago. When taken out of its pen, the bull was controlled with a metal staff attached to a copper ring in its nose.

The sale of milk (cream in the earlier years) provided some income monthly. Milk production was greatest in the early summer months when the cows were first put out to pasture. Most of the bull calves were kept and raised until they were six to twelve months old. Then they were sold for breeding purposes. One time we sold a record number of four calves in one week. Sometimes we sold cows to other farmers, when a representative of the county Shorthorn Breeders Association brought a prospective buyer to our farm. It was always somewhat exciting to know that such a buyer had come to look at our cows.

Some years, a bull calf would not be registered but would be raised until about a year old, when he was killed and butchered to provide meat, some used fresh and some canned. On rare occasions, a cow would be unproductive. In that case, she was sold to the butcher in Edgerton, who came to the farm, killed and dressed the animal, and took the carcass back to the butcher shop to be cut up and sold. The butcher always gave us a piece of the liver.

Every morning after milking, enough was taken to the house to meet my mother's cooking needs. No adult drank milk. I got my milk in the form of hot cocoa. We had no refrigeration and the cellar could not keep milk cool enough for me to like it. At every milking, the barn cats got some milk in a dish. Some of the milk had to be used for the young calves. When the milk was separated from the cream, they got skim milk. When we started to sell whole milk, they got a mixture of whole milk and water.

Calves were weaned from their mother when they were a few weeks old and taught to drink from a pail. Teaching a calf to drink was one of my tasks many times. I had to push the calf's head down into the milk, then dip my other hand in the pail and put my finger into the calf's mouth. The finger was a substitute for the mother's teat to fool it into drinking from the pail. In two or three days, the calf was drinking without this ruse.

When I was no more than six or seven, when the old cow barn was still in use, I teased my father to let me try to milk. I was too young. But by the time I was in high school, I was expected to help with the milking, night and morning, except on school days. The remodeled barn had stanchions for about twenty-eight animals. No more than thirteen or fourteen of those were being milked at any one time. The other stanchions were for "dry" cows (those not producing milk) or heifers. At milking time, I sat on a low wooden stool on the right side of the cow with the milk pail held between my legs. A few cows had a habit of kicking when being milked; I hoped they would not succeed in kicking over the pail or getting a foot in it. The pail was taken to the milk can at the end of the row of stanchions where the milk was poured into the can through a screen covered with cheesecloth. Milk cans held ten gallons, about eighty pounds.

After milk was being sold as whole milk, the can was taken to the milk house to cool. Every morning a truck picked up the milk and took it to a plant in Janesville. There, it was weighed, tested for butterfat, and then shipped to Chicago. Before that, when we sold cream, the container with cream was kept cool in the milk house until a horse-drawn wagon picked it up and took it to the creamery in Edgerton. Before being put in a big container on the wagon, the cream was weighed. One day, my mother was surprised to see a hired man, just employed to help for a few days, washing his face and hands with cream he had scooped from the can with his hands. That did not happen again!

In the 1920s, a new program required all cows in Wisconsin to be tested for tuberculosis. Some farmers lost all their herds. Some of our neighbors lost part of their herds, for which they received a small indemnity for each cow found to have tuberculosis and destroyed. Our herd was tuberculosis free. My father received a certificate from the U.S. Department of Agriculture or the Wisconsin Department of Agriculture and Markets, dated August 20, 1926, stating that he had an accredited tuberculosis-free herd. When any of our Milking Shorthorns were shipped out of state for breeding purposes, they had to be free of Bang's disease, which caused calves to be stillborn. The veterinarian from Edgerton who tested our animals had to stay all night because the test involved taking the animals' temperature every few hours. None of our animals were ever found to have Bang's disease. The only health problem for our cattle that I recall was the occasional case of bloat, when a cow ate something that gave her a bloated stomach. Rather than call the veterinarian, my father took care of this by piercing the cow's stomach with a knife to let out the air. As far as I can recall, they always recovered.

When a cow-testing association was organized in Rock County just for Shorthorns, my father joined. The association was promoted by the agricultural extension service as a management tool to identify the most profitable producing cows. Once a month, the cow tester, employed by the association, arrived in late afternoon and had supper with us. After supper, he went to the barn, weighed and recorded the milk from each cow, and took a small sample of milk. He stayed all night. In the morning, he repeated the process and got information as to what and how much each cow was fed. After breakfast, he set up his Babcock tester in the kitchen or on the back porch. The Babcock test showed the percentage of butterfat in the milk sample for each cow. He completed a record for each cow that showed her estimated monthly production of milk, butterfat, and feed consumption. Each month, Janesville's daily newspaper published a list of the top producers in the association, showing name of the owner, name of the cow, and the cow's milk and butterfat production. It was a matter of pride when the names of one or more of our cows appeared on the list. The American Shorthorn Breeders Association, of which my father was a member, also recognized high-producing cows with a Record of Merit Certificate. When I was old enough, I did the twice-a-day weighing of milk and kept the records sent in to qualify several of our cows for the Record of Merit award.

The cows were my favorite among the farm animals. By the time I was in high school, on Sunday mornings, I often took time to curry and brush them to make them look nice, especially on the Sundays when we had visitors. I knew the menfolk, after Sunday dinner, would go to the barn to look at the animals and talk.

Hogs

Hogs were an important source of income. We had Poland Chinas, a black hog kept by many Rock County farmers but outnumbered, in 1919, by the red Duroc Jersey. We always had six sows for spring litters. Some years, two or three sows had "fall pigs." At farrowing time, each sow was put where she could be by herself until after her pigs were born and for a while longer. On a few occasions, a sow ate her young.

When the pigs were about six weeks old, my father castrated the males with a sharply honed pocketknife. The pigs had some teeth that were black. My father removed these with pliers. I never understood the reason; perhaps he thought black teeth interfered with the pigs' eating. All the pigs had three or four copper hog rings in their snouts to prevent them from rooting up the fields. The hog rings were put in with a plier-like device especially designed for the purpose.

The sows were replaced each year. So was the boar. I remember my father going to the railroad station to pick up a boar he had purchased from a breeder some distance away. The young boar had been put in a slatted wooden crate for shipping.

When the pigs reached a weight of about two hundred pounds, they were sent off to market. In the early years, they were taken by wagon to a livestock dealer in Edgerton who would put them on a livestock car to be taken by train to a meat packer, most likely in Chicago. Later, a man who specialized in livestock hauling would come to the farm, when called. The pigs would be herded, squealing loudly, onto the truck and taken wherever my father requested—a small meat packer in Fort Atkinson, a larger one in Madison, or a still larger one in Chicago. Hogs were sold by the hundredweight. The farmer got what the packer offered on that day. There was no choice. The trucker brought the check back the same day or the next.

One or two hogs were butchered in the late fall for our use. First, a big, black cast-iron kettle, about twenty-four inches in diameter, was set up in the backyard and filled with water. A fire was built all around the kettle to bring the water to the boiling point. A heavy wooden platform, used to load cattle or hogs on a wagon or truck, was brought from its storage place in the corncrib and placed on two sturdy wooden sawhorses. Then the hog was killed with a hard blow to the skull. Next, its throat was cut to let out blood.

Butchering was a two-man task, done by my father and the hired man or a neighbor who was asked to help. If it was a neighbor, he always got a piece of liver to take home. After the hog was killed, a hog hook was inserted into each hind leg. Holding the hog hooks, the men pulled the hog back and forth in the kettle's hot water until the bristles softened. Then the hog was placed on the platform and the bristles removed with a hog scraper, a small metal tool.

After the organs inside the hog were removed, it was ready for my father to cut up. Some was cut to be used fresh, for example, the tenderloin—which I liked best of all—pork chops, and roasts. Some parts were cut to be made into salt pork, which, when fried, appeared frequently on our breakfast table; I never learned to like it. Some was for my mother to can. The hams were always smoked to the point where they could be kept in the cellar for a long time. Little went unused. Meat from the skull was made into headcheese, placed in small earthenware crocks, and stored in the cellar to be kept cool. It was served sliced and fried. I never liked it; it had too much fat. Sometimes the feet were pickled. Some years the intestines were cleaned to serve as the casing for sausage. The meat for the sausage was put in a grinder, to which was attached a metal spout. The casing was fitted over the spout. Turning the handle on the sausage grinder, which I sometimes was asked to do, forced the sausage meat into the casing. String was tied tightly around the filled casing every twelve or fifteen inches to make sausage links. The sliced and fried sausage was another frequent breakfast item in season.

The feared disease for hogs was hog cholera. Fortunately, our hogs never had it.

Sheep

We were the only ones in our neighborhood who had sheep. Ours were Shropshires, the breed kept by virtually all farmers in Rock County who had sheep in 1919. We had twelve to fifteen ewes. At lambing time, each ewe usually had one lamb, but there were always some who had two. On rare occasions, a ewe would disown her lamb. That lamb became mine to raise "on a bottle," meaning the lamb was fed warm milk from a bottle two or three times a day until it could be weaned. At this feeding stage, the lamb was always kept in the yard around the house. The lamb became a pet. When the lambs were a few weeks old, my father docked (cut off close to the body) their tails with his sharp knife. At the same time, the males were castrated. In spring, my father sheared all the adult sheep with sheep shears. Each fleece was placed in a "wool box," where it was compressed into a compact bundle held together with wool twine, a special brown, large-sized twine. The wool was sold, by the pound, to a dealer.

When the lambs had grown to a sufficient size they went to market, along with the sheep not kept for replacement. Every year we bought a new ram. It was not unusual to slaughter a lamb in the fall for us to eat.

I raised this lamb after its mother disowned it

About the time I was midway through grade school, we acquired two nanny goats, for reasons unknown to me. I got some milk from a nanny a time or two to see what goat milk tasted like; I did not keep up the practice. The nannies and their offspring were kept in the upper part of the barn, in the drive-in part where a team and loaded wagon could come in off the road. The young kids were mischievous. One day my grandmother and her husband came to visit and parked their big black touring car on the roadside opposite the barn. The kids escaped from the barn, and it was not long before three or four of them were up on the car's hood looking at their reflection in the windshield. Some of the kids, when big enough, were slaughtered and eaten like lamb.

From as early as I can remember, we kept a big horned billy goat to run with the cattle. I knew of no other farmer who had this practice. But my father believed that having a billy goat with the cattle was good for their health. The billy goat had a way of getting through the barbed wire fence that lined the lanes to the pastures. To stop this, a wooden yoke was put around his neck. One day, my father was carrying water to the sheep in their pen. When he was partway there, I saw the billy goat charging head down and full speed at my father's rear. I had no time to give warning. When hit, completely surprised, my father went sprawling, the two pails of water flying out of his hands. I never saw my father more angry. It was not long before the billy goat's horns were sawed off.

Chickens

Our chickens were Barred Plymouth Rocks, a general purpose breed that lay brown eggs. As of 1919, far more farmers kept this breed than kept White Leghorns. These had white eggs and, in time, became the most widely kept because of their egg production. Each year we selected about 100 to 125 hens along with 10 or 12 roosters. The roosters were kept to ensure that the hatching eggs needed in the spring would be fertile.

We had all the eggs we wanted to eat—fried, scrambled, boiled—and the eggs we marketed provided "grocery money." The eggs went to market in an egg crate with several layers, each separated by a strong cardboard-like piece. If the crate couldn't hold all the eggs, the rest went in a big dishpan of oats to prevent the eggs from being broken. Usually, at the store, every egg would be "candled," that is, held up to a light, to ensure that it was edible.

We often had chicken for Sunday dinner, especially when there were guests. My mother would catch the hen or rooster she wanted, place its neck on a chopping block (made of a chunk of wood), and cut off its head with a sharp ax. As soon as the chicken, headless, was placed on the ground, it would jump high in the air several times. Removing the feathers was facilitated by dipping the now-dead chicken into a pail of hot water. With the feathers off and the innards and feet removed, the bird was ready to be fried, roasted, or, if an old hen, stewed. Fall was the time to market the chickens we wouldn't keep over the winter. They traveled to market in chicken crates or, if there were too many, in gunny sacks, each chicken's head sticking out a hole cut in the sack for air. The chickens went to a dealer in a nearby town, most likely to be shipped to Chicago.

Our Barred Plymouth Rocks caught the fancy of some passersby or other people who knew about them. As a result, we were able to sell settings of eggs for hatching or roosters for breeding.

When I was perhaps nine or ten years old, I persuaded my mother to get a setting of Bantam chickens for me. I suppose I had seen these colorful, small chickens on display at the county fair. The eggs were too small to be marketable. The Bantams were not for eating. This project lasted only one year.

Once in a while, my mother would raise a few ducks for us to eat. We never had geese. The farm next to us always had a large flock of geese. When I was in high school, I had to pass this farm on my way to catch my ride to school. Often the geese were along the road when I passed by. Some of them always came at me, their necks stretched out and hissing. I had no liking for geese except when roasted and on the dinner table. We did not keep turkeys. The only farm in our neighborhood to keep turkeys was the one next to our schoolhouse. We had to go to this farm to get the water we used at school. When we appeared at the well, the three or four turkeys in sight would usually raise their tail feathers high and gobble loudly, somewhat frightening us young water carriers.

Dogs and Cats

Dogs and cats were a part of life on our farm. There was always a dog. The first one I knew was Ted, a good-sized dog of unknown breed. He was followed by my dog, Jack, a white Scotch Collie. Jack learned to get the cows from any part of the pasture and drive them into the lane that led to the barn. We only had to say, "Go get the cows," and Jack was off running at top speed. Except for two or three that stayed around the house, the cats made the barn their home. There they found plenty of mice to hunt. At one point, the cats multiplied to well over twenty, far more than wanted. Menfolk caught quite a number, put them in gunny sacks, and headed for Janesville in a buggy. Somewhere along the way, the howling cats were let out of the bags along the roadside.

5

Equipment

The wagon was the most frequently used major piece of equipment on the farm. It had multiple uses. With the wagon box in place, the wagon carried sacks of grain from the threshing machine to the granary, or barrels of water from the water tank to the beds where tobacco plants grew. With a "bang board" added to one side, it could carry the husked ripe ears of corn from the field to the corncrib. When the homemade hayrick was put on in place of the wagon box, it took hay to the barn, bundles of shocked grain to the threshing machine, and bundles of corn to the silo filler. At tobacco harvest time, a tobacco rack was put on to take the plants, on wood laths, to the tobacco shed. When we needed sand or gravel from the gravel pit, "stringers" from the tobacco shed replaced the wagon box. The stringers were the two-by-six-foot pieces of lumber on which tobacco laths were placed for the tobacco to cure. The load was dumped by turning the stringers on edge. Before we had a two-wheel trailer for our car, we used the wagon to take bags of grain or corn to the feed mill to be ground. The wagon wheels had to be greased to keep them from squeaking. When I was old enough, I liked to do the greasing. Each wagon wheel had a metal rim. At times, these rims would loosen and had to be taken to the blacksmith shop to be "set." When snow covered the ground, the bobsled took the place of the wagon.

Plows

If a field had been in hay, the first step in preparing it to be planted to corn was plowing. If the field had been in corn, it might be plowed or disked before planting to grain. We had three plows. The gang plow had two plowshares; it was pulled by three horses. The sulky plow, with one plowshare, was pulled by two horses. The walking plow was pulled by two horses. Only my father used the walking plow, which took a good deal of skill to use properly. I used both the gang plow and the sulky. I always enjoyed plowing, seeing the moist soil turn over in regular furrows, watching for the worms and grubs, which often attracted robins. When I was plowing, Robert Burns's poetry came to mind. At the end of each day, we greased the plow-shares to prevent rust. Every two or three years, a plowshare would hit a good-sized stone, left by the last glacier thousands of years ago, that had worked its way to the surface. The spot would be marked and the stone later removed.

We preferred to plow sod (the hayfields) in the fall to give the sod time to disintegrate before spring planting. In the spring, the plowed fields were gone over with a disk, pulled by three horses, to break up the soil for planting, and then with a spike-toothed drag, to break lumps and leave the soil level for planting.

Near one of the farm buildings stood a homemade roller, which could also break lumps. Seldom used, it had been made from a big log about two feet in diameter and ten feet long.

Planters

We planted grain with a grain seeder, which was perhaps ten feet long. From a box at the top of the seeder, the grain dropped through a set of funnels to be scattered on the ground and more or less covered by a set of shovels. Below the box on top was a much smaller box for clover and timothy seed. Sometimes, rather than using the seeder, the clover and timothy seed was sown by a hand-carried broadcast seeder, after the grain had been planted. Most farmers in the neighborhood used a grain drill that put the seed directly into the ground and covered it with soil. The seeder was cheaper. Only my father used the grain seeder.

The corn planter planted two rows at a time. It could be set for two methods of planting: drilled corn and checked corn. With drilled corn, the kernels were dropped at eight- to twelve-inch intervals. With checked corn, three or four kernels at a time were dropped in "hills," spaced at regular intervals. Checked corn required more skill to plant. Only my father did this. The advantage of the checked corn was that it could be cultivated in both directions.

Before starting to plant each two rows of corn, a heavy wire at least eighty rods long was anchored firmly in the ground at each end of the field. Traveling through an attachment to the corn planter, it had blobs of metal, spaced according to the distance between the hills of corn, that dropped the kernels. When the end of the field was reached, the wire had to be reset before starting back. Additionally, a pole-like device with a hoe-like end was dropped to the side of the corn planter at the beginning of each new row. This device marked where the next two rows of corn should be, if the driver followed the mark. After the corn was four or five inches high, we walked along the rows with a hand corn planter to add seed where the corn had not come up.

Planting tobacco with the tobacco setter required three persons. The driver of the team of horses pulling the setter sat on a seat attached to the barrel for water, which was up in front. In back and below, closer to the ground, were seats for two persons, one seat on each side of what would be the row of planted tobacco. Each person had a supply of newly pulled plants on a canvas apron. As the setter moved along, it made a clicking sound at regular intervals. At each click, water from the barrel came down a spout to the furrow, which had been made by the "shoe." The two persons doing the planting had a demanding and tiresome task; the tobacco setter moved at the horses' normal speed. The click was a signal. The two persons, in turn, had to have a plant ready so that at the click, the plant's roots could be placed where the water was dropped and the plant would be upright so the roots were immediately covered by the shoe. As soon as I was considered old enough, I was given the task. There could be a problem within a few days after planting. Cutworms in the soil had an uncanny ability to find the newly planted tobacco and cut the stem in two just below the soil's surface. So, a few days after planting was completed, we walked along each row, carrying a pail of replacement plants and a dibble (a short, round stick pointed at one end). When cutworm damage was found, we looked for the ugly-looking gray cutworm, killed it, took up the root of the original plant, and replaced it.

Cultivators

We had three riding cultivators. These were used mostly for corn, cultivating one row at a time. Cultivating started when the corn was four or five inches high and continued until it was about three feet high, about ready to tassel out. The shovels could be adjusted to cultivate to a certain depth and to direct the soil to cover weeds between hills of corn in the rows. Metal stirrup-like devices on either side enabled the driver to control the shovels.

We had two walking cultivators, one with shovels and the other with metal teeth. These were pulled by one horse. Cultivation of tobacco started with one of these walking cultivators within two or three days after planting was completed. Cultivation continued until the tobacco leaves were so large that they would be damaged if the horse and cultivator went between the rows.

Weeds that grew between the plants within the rows were removed by hoeing. At the end of each day's work, the hoes were oiled or greased to prevent rust. When hoeing the tobacco, we were on the lookout for tobacco worms—green with black markings. They could grow to be three or more inches long, with big bodies, and were voracious eaters of tobacco leaves. If not found and destroyed, they could severely damage the leaves.

Potatoes were cultivated with the shovel walking cultivator until the last cultivation, when a horse-hoe was used. It had blades that went along both sides of the potato row to "hill up" the potatoes.

Mowers, Binders, and Manpower

Hay was the first field crop to be harvested. The mower, pulled by two horses, cut a five-foot swath. Some birds made their nests in the hayfield, but I never saw a nest with eggs or baby birds. By hay-cutting time in June, very likely the eggs had hatched and the babies flown away. A few times, I did see the mower blade run over a nest of rabbits, too young to have left the nest. I never saw any of them injured but they had lost their cover. The scythe hanging in the barn was a reminder of the way all hay was cut before the invention and adoption of the mower. I learned to use the scythe to cut tall weeds and grass in out-of-the-way places on the grounds around the house and along the fence rows.

When my father first started to farm, the cut hay was gathered into piles with a horse-drawn dump rake. Then this hay was pitched onto the wagon and taken to the haymow or stack. But around the time the barn was remodeled, he bought a side-delivery rake and a hayloader. A few hours after the hay had been cut, to let it dry out, the side-delivery rake raked the hay into neat windrows. The hay loader was attached to the back of the wagon and the wagon was driven astraddle the windrow. The hayloader took the hay from the windrow and dropped it on the wagon. When I was old enough, I stood at the front of the wagon, driving the horses. My father always stood at the back of the wagon and distributed the hay on the back half of the wagon. The hired man was between me and my father. When the back half of the wagon was loaded, my father passed the hay to the hired man to load the other half. Loading the hay properly was important so the load did not tip over on the way to the barn. The hay had to be dry, free of dew or rain, before it could go in the haymow or stack. Wet hay could cause spontaneous combustion and a barn fire. We never had that experience, but more than once, when taking the hay out of the mow, I found a small area where the hay was gray because it had heated.

Grain harvest followed haying. The oats and other grains were cut with a grain binder usually pulled by three horses, except in very hot weather when two additional horses might be hitched ahead of the three. The binder's sickle cut, I think, a six-foot swath. As the stalks were cut, a rotating reel of wood pushed them onto a moving canvas. The canvas took the stems to the part of the binder where an ingenious device put the stems into a bundle and tied the bundle with binder twine. The bundle was then dropped to the side of the binder onto a fork-like catcher. When the catcher had as many bundles as it could hold, it released the bundles to the ground, at regular intervals. Then ten or so bundles were put into shocks, with one or two on top as a cap to keep out the rain. I was glad when I was old enough to drive the horses on the grain binder. Grain had to be cut at just the right time to get the maximum yield. If cut too soon, the kernels would be immature and lightweight. If cut too late, the kernels would shatter from the head as the grain was cut. The cradle hanging in the barn was a reminder of times past, before the grain binder was invented and adopted, when all the grain had to be cut by men with a cradle.

Tobacco harvest was between the grain and corn harvests. Tobacco harvesting was not mechanized. It was dirty, back-breaking, tedious work. It was dirty because a substance on the tobacco leaves left a black, gummy material on hands or gloves, on shirt-sleeves and over-alls. It was back-breaking and tedious because of the repetitious bending over required to harvest the thousands of plants in our five acres. The small plants set out in June grew rapidly to be about four feet high in August. Then the plants blossomed, a pinkish-white bloom. At this time, two or three weeks before harvest, the tobacco

My father on the grain binder

was "topped," that is, the blossom part with the small leaves just below was broken off. The tops were left on a few plants, which would provide seed for the next year's crop.

Harvest began when the color of the leaves indicated it was time. On the day of cutting, or two or three days earlier, each plant was "suckered." After topping, "suckers" began to grow at each node, the place where the leaf joined the stem. Suckers could get to be four or five inches long and had to be removed before the plant was cut. The biggest suckers were at the bottom of the plant; thus, one bent over to break them off. The plant was cut with a tobacco hatchet, at the ground level below the last leaf; this was another task that required bending. When the leaves had wilted enough to not be brittle, the stalks from about four rows were picked up and put into piles at intervals of perhaps a rod. This was another bending-over task that I was asked to do when I was too young to do the other steps in harvest. At these piles, the stalks were put on a tobacco lath using a "spud." The metal spud was pointed at one end; the other end was open to fit onto the wood lath. The pointed end pierced the stalks so they could be pulled on the lath. Five to seven stalks were put on the lath, depending on their size.

The lath with the stalks was laid on the ground to be picked up later and taken, on the tobacco rack, to the tobacco shed. There they hung until they were dried and "cured," ready for the leaves to be stripped off the stalk.

Corn was cut with the corn binder pulled by three horses, one row at a time. The binder bound the cut stalks, with binder twine, into bundles, which were dropped to the ground one by one. Corn for silage still had green stalks and leaves, the ears not fully mature. It was taken to the silo filler the same day it was cut, or within a day or two. Corn cut for its ears was not cut until the kernels were ripe, when the stalks were brown and the leaves were dry. The bundles for this corn were put into shocks. Later the ears were husked with a hand-held husking pin. The husked corn was either put directly into the wagon or put on the ground to be picked up later and taken to the corncrib. The bundles of stalks were taken to be stacked up along the barnyard. These bundles were put out in the barnyard for the cattle to eat when they were out of the barn for a few hours during the day. Some years, not all the corn was cut. The ripe ears would be husked right off the corn standing in the field and thrown into the wagon, which was moving parallel to the rows. Before the corn binder, all corn was cut with a corn knife. We used a corn knife to cut the

Stalks of tobacco on a lath to be taken to the curing shed (photo by John Onsud)

A load of tobacco being taken from the field to the curing shed

still-green sweet corn that was used to feed the cattle when pastures were short. My father always drove the corn binder. At corn-cutting time, I was in school except for the weekends. But I did shock corn and husk corn with the husking pin.

All the potatoes were dug by hand with a potato fork. In early July when potatoes were big enough to eat, we dug what was needed for daily use. Most of the crop was dug in the fall and stored in the cellar for use over the winter until the next year's crop was ready.

Other Equipment

The other large piece of equipment was the manure spreader, purchased after my father had been farming a few years. Every day, the barn had to be cleaned and the manure and bedding from cattle and horses put in a metal wheelbarrow and pushed outside to the manure pile. A few neighbors installed manure carriers in their barns. The manure remained in the pile until the "slack time" after hay harvest. Then it was pitched onto the manure spreader and taken to the field to be spread, with first priority to the recently cut hayfields. The manure from the pile had a strong odor that made it clear to all for some distance what was being done. The menfolk liked to call spreading the manure putting on the "prolific"! Before we had the spreader, the manure was put on the wagon and distributed manually with a fork. The manure spreader was laborsaving and distributed the manure much more uniformly.

There were numerous small pieces of equipment and tools. Some were used every day, some only a few times a year or less.

The swill barrel was used twice a day during the part of the year when the hogs were not confined to their pen. It was a large barrel mounted on the platform of a two-wheeled cart. The cart would be pulled to the water tank, filled with water pail by pail, then pulled to the hog troughs. After ground feed was added, the liquid mixture would be poured into the troughs to be consumed by the squealing pigs.

The stone boat, used a couple of times a year if that, was hand-made with a base of two split logs ten or twelve feet long over which boards were nailed to make a platform. The stone boat was used to move large stones from the field.

The large grindstone, turned with pedals like a bicycle, was used to sharpen axes. The flail hanging in the barn was a reminder of the days before the threshing machine. It separated kernels of ripe grain, especially wheat or other grains used for food, from the heads. It consisted of a wooden handle to which was attached by thong or rope a shorter, stouter stick. We used the flail only to separate dry beans or peas from their pods.

When we went to the woods to cut down trees for firewood, we took axes, a cross-cut saw, a bucksaw, metal wedges, and a sledge hammer. First, we cut a notch near the base of the tree with an ax to determine the direction the tree should fall. Then, with one person at each end of a cross-cut saw, we cut through the tree from the other side until the tree fell. We trimmed branches with axes, cut off the trunk with the bucksaw, and sawed the log into shorter lengths. We used a wedge and a sledge hammer to split the larger pieces. We piled these logs and branches near the house. Then a neighbor with a buzz saw came and sawed the logs and branches into pieces short enough to use in the living room stove, or he split them into smaller pieces for the kitchen stove.

When we built or repaired a fence using wood posts, we took a posthole digger, a shovel to put the soil back around the post, and the tamper to compact the soil firmly around the post. We used a maul to drive in steel posts. If woven wire was used, we used a wire-stretcher to tighten the wire before attaching it to the post.

We had various forks and shovels. We used pitchforks to handle hay, to toss bundles of grain from the shock onto the wagon, and to move the bundles from the wagon onto the threshing machine. We had a manure fork, a silage fork, and a straw fork. Shovels included a long-handled one for digging, a manure shovel for cleaning out the barn, a grain shovel for filling bags in the granary, and a scoop shovel for throwing ears of corn from the wagon into the corncrib.

Other equipment included a brush hook to cut brush, a hand sprayer to rid the potatoes of potato bugs, a crowbar to move objects, and a pinch bar to loosen objects. For working with wood, we had a cross-cut saw and a ripsaw, an adze for shaping wood, a plane for smoothing wood, an auger for drilling holes, a level, and a square.

For repair work, we had a large vise, pliers, chisels, files, and a variety of wrenches—crescent, monkey, and pipe. We had stepladders, especially for cherry-picking time, and long wooden ladders whose use included getting on the roof of the house to put out chimney fires.

We had a scale with a platform. The scale could weigh things up to several hundred pounds. When I was in 4-H Club, each month, with the help of my father, I would get my calf on the scale to weigh it.

The Economics of the Farm

All income from the farm was divided equally between my father and the Walraths, except for the sale of eggs and chickens. My mother received the money from the eggs and chickens. However, the Walraths could have all the eggs they wanted and whatever chickens they wanted to eat.

My father paid for the hired labor, the horses, and the farm equipment. Mr. Walrath was responsible for the real estate taxes, the upkeep of buildings, and new fencing. Some costs were divided equally, for example, the threshing.

There was always discussion about the price received for items sold, for example, the price per pound for tobacco, the price per hundredweight for hogs, the price for every registered cow sold, and the price for a dozen eggs. My mother kept some type of record of the income, but I never saw the records and I never heard mention of our annual income. I suppose that the gross farm income never exceeded fifteen hundred dollars in the best of years.

My folks never borrowed money and never bought on credit. When we bought our first car for about five hundred dollars, the money was there to pay for it. Likewise, when we bought a new horse for two hundred dollars or a new piece of machinery, it was paid for in full.

My parents had a checking account at one of the local banks and a savings account at both of the banks. In the early 1920s they had saved enough money that my father could loan my mother's uncle eighteen hundred dollars to build a new house. My father held a mortgage on the house. The uncle paid interest and repaid the loan in full in about ten years. My father also had an ordinary life insurance policy for a thousand dollars.

A few larger farms in the neighborhood kept more cows for milk or raised more tobacco and undoubtedly had more farm income than we did. But I think our farm did as well as most of our neighbors and better than some.

6

Hired Men

During the busy season, from planting through harvest, my father could not do all the farm work by himself, so he took on a hired man, paid by the month. These men were always single. They ate their meals with us and had a room of their own, and my mother did their laundry with the family wash. Sometimes additional help, paid by the day, was hired for short periods, such as tobacco harvest.

During the time I was at home, most of the men hired by the month were relatives. The first hired man I remember was my mother's youngest brother, Uncle Fred. He had lived with his widowed mother and stepfather on a farm until, at about the age of sixteen or seventeen, he came to work for my father. From that time until he was married, our home was his home. One of the things he did soon after joining us was to buy a sled for me. This sled never wore out. Another thing he did was buy a bicycle, which he stored where our car was. I would go in by myself to admire it, wishing I could ride it. I never did get to ride, but actually I was too small to do so. Later, Uncle Fred bought a horse and buggy; the horse soon died. One winter, my uncle went to Janesville and worked in a tobacco warehouse; he did not like it. For two years or so he left to work for another farmer on a very good farm. But he came back to be with us.

One day during tobacco harvest when he, my father, and I were hanging tobacco in the tobacco shed, he said, blushing, that he was going to start farming for himself. That meant that he was going to get married. My father immediately said that he would loan Uncle Fred five hundred dollars to help get started and named a piece of farm equipment he could have. Uncle Fred started out as a farm tenant. Before long, when he was a tenant on a very productive 120-acre farm, all tillable, the owner decided to sell the farm. A wealthy farmer nearby voluntarily offered my uncle the money to buy the farm; he had noticed what a good farmer and hard worker my uncle was.

Another of my mother's brothers, Uncle Paul, also worked for my father but did not overlap with Uncle Fred. One day, at the noon meal, he said that he "wanted to put his feet under his own table." That meant that he was going to get married and start farming for himself. He was always a renter.

The third relative to work for my father was my mother's nephew, my cousin. He had been sent by his father who had a small farm in the cutover area of northern Wisconsin. My cousin started working on our farm the first year I was in college so we worked together the summer after my first year away.

One year, when my uncles no longer worked for us, the hired man was a recent emigrant from Norway. Another year, my father was persuaded to take a young man, a relative of my father's sister's husband's family in Norway, who had a drinking problem. His family thought sending him to work on a farm in America might help him get over his problem. He was a greenhorn with respect to our type of farming. The one thing I remember about him is that one morning he went to the pasture to fetch the cows for milking. In the gully at the end of the lane he noticed what he thought was one of our black and white cats caught in a trap. I had set the trap for woodchucks. When he went to take the cat out of the trap, it turned out to be a skunk, about which he knew nothing. The skunk thoroughly sprayed him. He came back to the barn with the cows. All the milk had to be discarded because of the skunk odor. All the clothes he had on were buried in the manure pile.

The persons I recall being hired by the day included a neighbor boy who helped with the tobacco setting one year, a man hired to help with haying and with tobacco harvest, and the man and wife on the neighboring farm who often helped with tobacco stripping.

One man, Nick, was a "standby" for work by the month and by the day. He was about my father's age, unmarried, and made his home with his unmarried brother, who had his own farm. Nick sometimes bought the *Chicago Daily Tribune* to read on Sunday. He let me have the comic section. There I got introduced to my favorite comics, such as *The Katzenjammer Kids* and *Bringing Up Father* ("Jiggs and Maggie"). Every three weeks or so, Nick would go to town with us on a Saturday night. When it was time to go home, he could not be found. He would go on a weekend drinking binge. Two or three days later, after he sobered up, he would show up at the farm ready to go back to work.

When I was twelve years old, a neighbor called my parents to ask if I could help him with haying by driving a horse on the hayfork. I was paid one dollar a day. As I got older, I helped a next-door neighbor several times with haying. I was paid two dollars a day. One time I helped him clean out the hog pen. When I was in high school, I helped another neighbor hoeing tobacco, haying, and harvesting tobacco. I received five dollars a day for tobacco harvest. The year after finishing high school, one of my best friends grew tobacco to get money for college. My friend hired me to help harvest and strip the tobacco. Because of the distance of his farm from ours, I stayed overnight with my friend's family when doing this work.

Only a few of our neighbors regularly had a hired man on a monthly basis for part of the year or year-round. The others had enough family labor on the farm or were small enough so that they got by with some help hired by the day. The most memorable of these hired men was the one whose real name I did not know for a long time. I heard the adults refer to him as Humdinger, I suppose because of his tall tales. He was the hired man for an elderly couple, retired from active farming, whose son lived on the adjoining farm. Humdinger seemed to be the decision maker with respect to day-to-day activities on the farm. He was invited to the social events in the neighborhood. When our country school held a box social to raise money, he would be the auctioneer. At the school's Christmas program, Santa Claus was always expected to appear with a sack of gifts. As I grew older, I figured out that the man in the Santa Claus suit had to be Humdinger. The longtime hired man on another farm developed tuberculosis and died. Later, that farmer, for a time, had a mentally retarded young man from one of the state institutions. Another farm had an older man, who stayed with the family for years. He had something of a drinking problem.

During the year between finishing high school, in 1927, and starting college, in 1928, I was the hired man. I had hoped that my father would consider this year an opportunity to visit his family in Norway. He had not been back since he came to the United States in 1903. My secret agenda was that if he went to Norway, I could be in charge of the farm. He did not go.

In my first summer out of high school, I worked for an elderly neighbor, in poor health, who needed help to get the hay harvested on his small farm. I hired one of my high school friends and used my father's mower, wagon, and team of horses. My friend stayed with us until the job was done.

The summer after my first year in college, I went back to help for the summer. My father said he would pay me seventy-five dollars a month; this was above the going rate. After the summer of 1928, my work on the farm was limited to what I did on weekend visits or vacation visits.

The hired men on our farm and in the neighborhood all had farm backgrounds, with a few exceptions. Some were upwardly mobile on the "agricultural ladder," becoming tenants and then farm owners. Others were lifetime hired laborers, some on a year-round basis, and others on a day or seasonal basis.

7

Patterns of Work and Farm Life

Work and life on the farm were shaped by the seasons, in a cycle repeated year after year after year. Within the seasonal cycle were a daily pattern and a weekly pattern, repeated throughout the year.

The Seasonal Cycle

When winter snows melted and the frozen ground thawed and the robins returned from the south, we knew spring was at hand. Preparations for spring's work had already been made. The harnesses had been washed in warm water, oiled, and repaired if necessary, and the brass parts polished. Oats and other grain to be used for seed had been put through the fanning mill to blow out the light kernels and leave the heavy kernels for planting. Plowshares had been taken to the blacksmith for sharpening. All the potatoes left in the cellar had their sprouts removed so the potatoes would be edible until the new crop was ready.

In early spring, the ewes lambed and the sows farrowed. It took two or three weeks before all the ewes had their lambs. The newborn lambs and the ewes were checked carefully to be sure no ewes had disowned their lambs. If a lamb died, it might be skinned and the pelt put over a disowned lamb, which was then put with the ewe whose lamb had been lost. It could be quite cold at lambing time, so weak lambs would be brought to the house, wrapped in a cloth, and put in front of the kitchen stove for a few hours to be kept warm and gain strength.

When about to farrow, each sow was separated from the other pigs and kept with her litter for a few days after they were born. A litter of six, seven, or eight was hoped for. Calves arrived throughout the year, although it seemed there were a few more in the spring than during the other seasons. In spring, hens started to get "broody." As many of the broody hens as were needed were put by themselves with a setting of eggs that the hen sat on for the twenty-one days to hatching time. After all the chicks were hatched, the hen and chicks were placed in a small A-shaped house where they stayed all night until the chicks were big enough to be on their own. The broody hens not needed for hatching eggs might be plunged headfirst into the water tank. This cold water treatment usually got them over their broodiness and back to laying eggs.

Oats were planted as soon as the soil was dry enough to be worked. The earlier the oats were planted, the better the yield was expected to be. Other grains followed the oats.

Around the time of Good Friday, my father put a cupful of tobacco seeds, which were very tiny, into a wool sock. The sock was moistened with warm water and placed in a pan near the kitchen stove. The sock was kept moist. When the seeds sprouted, they were sown in a carefully prepared tobacco bed where they grew until big enough to be transplanted in the field. Our tobacco bed was always in a new location each year, in a pasture plowed the previous fall. In the spring, this plot was worked into good tilth. Raised beds were made with a rake about three feet wide and perhaps twenty feet long. When the seeds in the sock had germinated, the sock was taken to the new bed. One tablespoon of the sprouted seeds was put in a sprinkling can of water. Can by can, the seeds were applied until all the beds had their seeds. Then a light layer of sand was spread over each bed to help keep the weeds to a minimum. By mid-June, the plants were big enough to be set in the field. Most tobacco-growing neighbors started their plants in the same location year after year. But before the seeds went into the beds, the soil was steamed to kill the weeds. The steaming was done with special equipment attached to a steam engine that traveled from farm to farm. Usually these beds were covered with white cloth over a wood frame.

My father always said that the time to plant corn was "when the leaves on the oak trees were as big as squirrels' ears." This was in early May.

When the pasture grass was green and ready, the cattle were turned out to pasture and no longer kept in the barn at night, and the horses were let loose to go to the pasture after the day's work.

Other spring activities included shearing the sheep, planting the garden, and planting the potatoes, with pieces of potatoes having at least one eye. The men stored the living room stove in a closet for the summer, and my mother cleaned the chimney.

Spring was also the time when the fruit trees blossomed, filling the air with fragrance and attracting the buzzing, busy bees gathering nectar for honey. Every year a pair of wrens tried day after day to build their nest in the clothespin bag that hung on a post on the back porch.

June was tobacco planting time. Late June was haying time, usually completed by the first part of July. After unloading hay on a hot day, we were always glad when my mother came out with a pitcher of cool lemonade and cookies before we went back for another load. Then it was time to clean the manure out of the barnyard before grain harvest.

With the hot days of summer came the flies, a problem in the barn and house. Flies came into the barn with the cows at milking time. Behind the cows and horses, dozens of white maggots squirmed on the floor. At the house, the odors of food attracted swarms of flies to the screen door leading into the kitchen. My mother always had a fly-shooer outside the door, which consisted of long strips of newspaper tacked to an old broomstick. When entering the kitchen at fly time, we were supposed to shoo the flies away before opening the door. Nevertheless, some got in, so strips of fly paper were hung around the kitchen; flies couldn't get free of the sticky surface if they landed on it. And fly swatters were always at hand.

By late June or early July, on workday evenings, after the men had finished the evening chores and my mother had cleaned up the kitchen and washed the dishes after supper, everyone gathered on the back porch steps. This was a time to relax after a day of hard work, to talk about the weather, the crops, and any other topic that came up. On early July evenings, with perhaps a light breeze stirring the air, I often heard my father say, "I can hear the corn grow." Before I was twelve, still going barefoot in summer, I had to get a basin of water and wash my feet before going to bed.

In my early years, grain threshing was done in the fall, sometimes as late as November. At that time, a traveling threshing rig went from farm to farm. This rig had a coal-fired steam engine (we supplied the coal) and a crew of three men. The crew always stayed with us one night. There was an informal mutual aid agreement, each farmer understanding that he would help the others.

Later on, grain harvest took place in the later part of July and early August. By the time I was in country school, threshing was done in August. Instead of using a traveling rig, the bundles of grain were taken directly from the shocks in the field to the threshing machine, run by a long belt attached to a tractor. The grain, after being measured automatically so the thresher and farmer would know how many bushels were threshed, came down the metal spout to be bagged and taken to the granary in the barn. The straw came out of a blower and was built into a stack. Stacking was a dirty job always done by my father. When I was old enough, I was given the job of handling the blower to direct the straw where my father wanted it.

A large crew was required for threshing "out of the shock": five or six men, each with a team and wagon, to take the bundles of grain from the field to the threshing machine; three in the field to pitch the bundles onto the wagons; one to handle the blower; the "bagger"; and three to load the bags of grain on the wagon, take them to the granary, and then unload them. My mother had a sizable crew to feed for at least one noon meal and sometimes for supper.

My first job at threshing time was to take a jug of water to the field for the men who were working as pitchers. Everyone drank out of the same jug. I took the jug to the field in a cart pulled by my pony. Before everyone began to thresh "out of the shock," the shocked grain was taken to one location and put into cylindrical stacks spaced so that the threshing machine could get between them.

Tobacco harvest came after grain harvest. It took a week or ten days to get the five acres of tobacco in the sheds.

After we got a silo, silo filling came next. The silo filler, run by a long belt attached to a tractor, was owned by one of the neighbors. Our silo was filled in one day. The crew included five or six men with teams to bring the cut corn bundles to the silo filler, two or three men to help load the wagons, and someone inside the silo to distribute the finely cut stalks and ears and "tramp" it down. As soon as I was old enough, I was inside the silo either with my father or by myself. My mother had a crew to feed on silo-filling day.

In September, the ears on the corn were mature and the kernels dry, so the corn was cut and the bundles put into shocks. The ears were later husked and taken to the corncrib. The bundles of stalks were put in a stack close to the barnyard where they were fed to the cattle when they were outside on winter days.

Fall was a time for picking up "windfall" apples and taking them to the cider mill. It was a time to dig the potatoes and to pick "winter" apples and store them in the cellar, along with dry onions, beets, and carrots. It was a time to pick up nuts from under the hickory trees along the roadside and in the woods and from under the three black walnut trees in the yard. This was the time when all the livestock began again to stay in the barn or in their pens all night. And this was the time for fall plowing.

Fall was also the time to market spring pigs, when they had grown to weigh about two hundred pounds (the brood sows had been sold earlier). Some lambs and ewes were sold. And all the chickens not to be kept for laying hens or breeding roosters went to market. Before cold weather set in, all the chickens we would keep were put in the henhouse. Late fall was also the time to butcher one or two of the spring pigs for family consumption.

Tobacco stripping could come any time between late November and late January or early February. It all depended on when "case" weather came after the green leaves had been "cured," that is, were brown in color and dry. Case weather was damp weather, rain or fog, which softened the leaves so the plants could be handled without the leaves breaking into pieces. When case weather came, it was urgent to take down the tobacco plants, which had been hanging on laths since harvest, and put the laths with the plants into piles, leaf tips toward the center of the pile. The leaves would remain soft and pliable for some time. My father always put the "hands" of leaves into the bundle—special tobacco wrapping paper placed in a specially made box with notches for the right number of pieces of the tobacco twine used to tie the full bundle. Stripping usually took about ten days with at least four people at work. I helped with stripping when old enough, but my principal task was to do all the chores except milking so that my father could keep stripping. I also helped carry out the stalks, now free of leaves, and loaded them on the wagon to be taken to the field and spread. If I was in the stripping area when a bundle was filled, I sometimes carried it to the tobacco shed where the bundles were kept until delivered to the buyer.

After tobacco stripping was out of the way, when the weather was not snowy or too cold, we could go to the woods at our convenience to cut enough trees for a year's supply of firewood. After the logs and branches had been cut into stove-length chunks, a good part of the chunks were split into smaller pieces for the kitchen stove. I split and piled a lot of wood.

Rainy Days and Holiday Interruptions

Rain put a halt to all work in the field. If rain came when we were in the field, we headed to the barn, put the horses in their stalls, and sat in the barn watching the rain come down. If it rained all day, we could do little except the necessary chores and odd jobs that could be done inside. The all-day rains provided the only chance to take a daytime nap in the haymow.

After rain, before we could resume work in the field, was a time to cut or pull weeds. A few Russian thistles, tall with purplish blossoms, grew along the fence or in the pasture, as well as burdock. The one major noxious weed was Canada thistle, which could grow in the grain fields. We tried to cut out Canada thistles before they blossomed. At one point, we had some quack grass in a field for crops. One year we dug the quack grass, loaded it on a wagon, and took it to a nearby elderly farmer who welcomed having it unloaded on his hilly pastureland. Horseradish was not technically a weed, but became such in a part of the orchard. Decades before my parents moved to the farm, the Walraths had planted horseradish in the orchard. The white roots were grated to make a condiment. But the initial planting spread and spread to take over the ground in a large part of the orchard. So, one year, we dug up all the horseradish and took it to the same farmer who took the quack grass. We were fortunate in not having the velvet weed, which was found on some neighboring farms. The differences in soil type probably explained why velvet weed did not grow in our fields.

Another job after rainy days was to walk along the rail fences to see if any rails had been pushed over or if the wooden braces at each zigzag of the fence were firmly in place.

July Fourth was the only holiday when we didn't work in the field. We did not stop work for Memorial Day, Labor Day, or, after it started, Armistice Day. Thanksgiving, Christmas, and New Year's were off season for outside work. On one Fourth of July, a day when we usually went to Milton for the daytime part of the celebration, we were behind schedule in haying. My father decided that we should work that morning to get in the hay; I was much disappointed. One year, case weather came on Thanksgiving Day, unusually early.

Mother's Work and the Seasonal Cycle

The seasons also influenced my mother's work, some related to the activities described for planting and harvesting and the livestock, others independent of those.

In spring, the seasonal influence started with the broody hens, the selection of some to hatch eggs, and then the raising of the chicks. Nearly every year, one or two hens would build a nest in tall grass or weeds, unknown to anyone until she appeared with her chicks. The only enemy of the young chicks was the weasel. If the hen set off a big disturbance during the night, it was a sure sign that a weasel had gotten into the coop. When my mother or father rushed out, it would always be too late. Five or six chicks were dead, their blood sucked out by the weasel.

Another spring task was planting the garden and caring for it through the last vegetable harvest. Every morning at tobacco planting time, my mother helped pull plants for the day's setting. At haying time, she drove the horse on the hayfork if Porter or I was not available. Canning was underway before that, starting with the rhubarb pulled from the rhubarb patch. Then came the picking of the strawberries (with some help) for sauce and jam. Picking red currants for jelly came about the same time as picking red cherries (with some help) for canning.

In August, when the blackberries were ripe in a nearby farmer's woods, she would don overalls, tied tight at the bottom, and put mosquito netting over her head and face. She would come back with two milk pails full of blackberries for jam. At tobacco harvest, my mother always did her part in spudding tobacco (putting the stalks on the wood lath). She would stop in the field an hour before noon to get dinner and an hour before suppertime to prepare the evening meal. When apples were ready in the fall, she did most of the picking up of windfalls and off the tree for applesauce and apple butter. Throughout the summer, it seemed that there was almost always some type of fruit or vegetable to can or preserve. Sometimes the food preservation involved cutting kernels of sweet corn off the cob and drying them in the sun. The dried kernels were used with milk added.

Also, apples were pared and sliced and the slices strung on strings. The strings were put out in the sun to dry the apples, for later use.

When cold weather came she selected which chickens to send to market and which to keep. With the fall butchering of hogs, she smoked the hams and shoulders, canned some of the meat, and made headcheese and sometimes sausage. When it was time to strip tobacco, she always helped. On some winter evenings, she cracked the hickory nuts and walnuts gathered in the fall. She cracked the nuts with a hammer on a piece of railroad iron about six or seven inches long. The nutmeats had to be picked from shells for use in cookies and cakes. I usually was asked to help with this.

On rare occasions in the winter, the cream or milk was not picked up if snow had made the roads impassable. Then my mother would get out the churn and make butter. I usually was asked to turn the crank on the churn. It usually seemed a long time before the cream turned into butter, ready to be taken out and put into molds or bowls. The darning of socks and the mending of work clothes were never-ending jobs, usually done in the evening, and unrelated to the seasons.

Daily Patterns

Some parts of the daily patterns of work and life stayed the same throughout the year. But some activities in the busy, demanding planting, cultivating, and harvesting months differed from those in the less busy late fall and winter months. A few activities were different when the livestock were confined to the barn at night during the colder months from when they were out of the barn at night on pasture. And a few differed according to whether the kitchen and living room stoves were in use.

Every day someone had to take care of the livestock. There were cows to be milked twice a day, every day of the year. The cattle had to be fed twice a day when not on pasture. The bull and calves were never on pasture so they had to be fed twice a day. When the horses were working, they were fed three times a day; other times, they were fed twice a day except when they were on pasture. Sheep were fed twice a day except when on pasture. Hogs and chickens were fed twice a day. All the livestock had to have water. The cows and horses could drink from the water tank, but someone had to carry water in pails to the bull, the calves, the sheep, and the chickens. The hogs got their water with the swill twice a day. When silage was fed, someone had to climb the ladder once a day to get into the silo. (This ladder was in an enclosed area between the barn and the silo.) Using a silage fork, he threw down enough silage for the after-milking morning feeding and the before-milking evening feeding. To get the horses fed twice a day, almost every day someone had to climb the ladder into the haymow and pitch the hay down the chute. When the cattle and horses were confined to the barn, the manure had to be cleaned out daily and straw brought in from the stack close to the barn for fresh bedding. My mother or I gathered eggs each afternoon. At the house, pails of water had to be brought daily from the well for drinking and cooking.

What was the repetitive pattern generally like each day from getting up in the morning until bedtime in the evening? In the busy season, my father got up at 5:00 a.m., called the hired man to get up, and started a fire so it would be ready for my mother to get breakfast. The first task in the barn was milking. If the cows were in the pasture, someone had to get them; I liked to do this when I was barefoot and could feel the dew on the grass and enjoy the fresh morning air. After milking, the can (or cans) was taken to the milk house to stand in cool water until it was picked up to be taken to the milk plant in Janesville. When the cattle were confined overnight, they were fed silage, grain, and hay. During the busy season, the horses were curried, brushed, and harnessed. Before whole milk was sold, the milk separation was done before breakfast. Each morning, my father took enough milk to the house to meet my mother's needs for cooking. Breakfast was always ready when the men came from the barn. It was always a hearty meal: fried potatoes, usually salt pork or eggs, bread, sometimes oatmeal or cream of wheat, coffee, and always dessert, be it cookies, cake, sauce, or pie. After breakfast someone, usually my mother but me when I was available, had to take the pail from the pantry to the well and refill it. This water was used for drinking and cooking.

After breakfast, the men headed back to the barn. When the livestock were confined, the hogs were given their swill, the sheep were fed and watered, the horses were taken to the tank for water, and the barn was cleaned. In the busy season, we were often working in the field by 7:00 a.m., weather permitting. We could not bring hay or cut grain that was wet with dew or rain. After breakfast, my mother fed and watered the chickens and proceeded with preparing the noon meal or her other work.

The men came in at noon for dinner, after watering and feeding the horses, in the busy season. Dinner was the heartiest meal of the day: meat, potatoes, vegetables, bread, dessert, and coffee (left over from breakfast). Someone might check the mail. My father carried water to the calves and the bull.

In the busy season, we were back in the field by about 1:00 p.m. and worked there until about 5:00 p.m. or later. The horses were watered, unharnessed, and fed and, if the cattle and sheep were confined, they were fed. If the sheep were on pasture, they would be brought to their pen overnight. Before preparing supper, my mother would have fed the chickens and gathered the eggs. We had supper at about 6:00 p.m. This meal almost always included meat, potatoes, bread, some type of vegetable, dessert, and tea. After supper, the cows were milked, the calves fed, and the hogs swilled. The hogs also got an abundant supply of ear corn. When the kitchen stove and the living room stove were in use, someone had to fill the woodbox for split wood, which was on the back porch, and take chunks of wood for the living room stove to the back porch. Most evenings, my father would sit in the rocking chair in the kitchen and smoke his one cigarette a day. He was in bed, during the busy season, by about 8:00 p.m. The rest of us were in bed by 9.

Weekly Patterns

No field work was done on Sunday, even in the busy season, but all the chores with the livestock had to be taken care of as on other days. In the summer, Sunday morning was the time for my father to mow the lawn, with a hand mower, if the grass needed cutting. I liked to take a pail of salt to the pasture and spread it for the cattle to lick. Sunday was the day for any visiting with relatives, usually my mother's three brothers, three or four times a year. Either we went to their place for Sunday dinner or they came to ours. We also went to my grandmother's house three or four times a year, usually for dinner.

Monday was washday for my mother. A big, copper tub filled with water was heated on the kitchen stove and used for washing clothes. In cold weather, the washer was brought into the kitchen; in warm weather, it was on the porch. This washer was a wooden tub mounted on legs. A stick-like handle moved a paddle-like device that agitated the clothes until they were judged to be clean. Then they were put through a hand-cranked wringer attached to the washer. Whenever she could, my mother recruited me to push and pull the handle on the machine and to crank the wringer while she inserted the wet clothes. This was one of my least favorite tasks. After the clothes went through the wringer, she hung them on the clothesline in the yard to dry in the sun. This was fine in nice weather; the clothes came off the line smelling fresh. But in cold weather, the sheets and other things sometimes came off the clothesline frozen stiff. Then they had to be thawed out in the house. For some reason, we often had baked potatoes for dinner on washday

Tuesday was ironing day, and one midweek day was baking day. The dough for bread was started the night before in a big metal container with a cover. By morning, the yeast would bring the dough to the top of the container. Baked in the kitchen stove oven, the loaves came out brown on top with a wonderful aroma—enough for a week's supply. Cookies were usually oatmeal, white sugar, or chocolate. Pies and cakes were made for more special occasions, such as Sunday dinner or threshing crew meals. Once in a while, my mother made doughnuts. I was always glad when I came home from country school and found fresh doughnuts.

On Saturdays during the busy season, when the weather was fairly warm, work in the field stopped about an hour earlier than on other days. Chores were done early and supper was early. This gave time for the men to shave, bathe, and put on clean clothes and for my mother to get ready to go to Edgerton. My mother took the eggs to a grocery store to exchange for groceries. After their shopping, families walked up and down the main street, meeting and visiting with friends and neighbors. My father usually stopped by the International Harvester machinery dealer to talk with the owners. When I was in high school, I would meet my three close friends at the public library and then go to the movies. Sometimes my mother bought a quart of ice cream, which was getting soft by the time we got home, but the treat was appreciated. During the less-busy season, weekly shopping was done in the daytime.

A few other things had to be done but not as regularly as the Sunday, Monday, Tuesday, Saturday schedule. Every ten days or two weeks, grain had to be bagged and taken to the feed mill to be ground for cows and hogs. This trip took several hours with team and wagon, but after we had a car with a trailer, it took less time. A regular task for my mother was caring for the kerosene lamps, our source of artificial light. They had to be refilled with kerosene, the wicks trimmed, and the chimneys washed to rid them of the soot.

8

Transportation and Communication

Roads

For years, a dirt road went past our farm to the country school. After wet weather, wagon wheels made ruts so the road was rough to drive on. The Town of Fulton bought road scrapers, and one of these was often left at our place. It consisted of two strong metal pieces, one in front and one in back, held together with a platform on top. When the ruts were bad, my father would hitch a team of horses to the scraper and fill in the ruts from our place to the school. I think he was paid one dollar each time he did this. It was a way of "working off" the town taxes. When I was old enough, I got to do this job. Later the town government decided that the road would be graveled. A gravel pit was opened in our pasture on the house side of the road, and gravel was hauled by team and wagon from the pit to the road. My father and our neighbors did all of this work, shovelful by shovelful.

In winter, there were no snowplows to clear the road. If the drifts were deep at certain points, they would be shoveled clear by men who lived along the road. When there were not drifts, my father attached a walking plow to the bobsled and cleared the snow. On occasions when a deep drift had not yet been made passable, we reached our place by taking down a fence and crossing one of our fields with team and bobsled. In spring, a part of the road near the school that was low lying was sometimes washed out in spots and impassable. Then, everyone drove through a neighbor's field.

The other road that passed the school (the road I did not walk on to school) was a state highway. When I first knew it, this was a gravel road, but when I was in country school, it was made into a two-lane concrete road. At lunchtime and recess, we could watch construction crews of men and horses moving earth from higher areas to fill in lower areas for an even, level road. All the earth was moved by horse-drawn dump shovels. There was no other earth-moving equipment in sight.

Building a concrete road was a somewhat controversial issue for the people in the area. This prompted our teacher to have some of the pupils debate the issue, pro and con. I was on the team against the concrete road. One of my arguments was that driving horses to town on this hard surface would cause injury to their hooves and legs.

Cars

Before we got our first car, a Ford Model T, in 1926, we got to town or elsewhere by horse and buggy, team and wagon, horse and cutter, or team and bobsled.

About a month after we got the car, we drove it to the county fair in Janesville and parked on the fairgrounds. When we went to go home in late afternoon, the car was not there. It had been stolen. It was never recovered. Another Model T replaced it.

My father drove a horse and buggy before he bought his first car in 1926

With snow in winter, we did not use the car. The radiator was drained, and the car put up on blocks so the tires were not touching the ground. There it sat until roads were passable in the spring.

A Ford Model T was started with a hand crank. Cranking could be hazardous. The crank would sometimes "kick"; breaking an arm when cranking a car was fairly common. We escaped that misfortune. Two levers on the steering wheel, one for gas and the other for ignition, had to be adjusted properly to start the engine. The driver used floor pedals to put the car into gear to move forward, to put the car into reverse, and to brake it to a stop.

Two of my uncles with an early model car owned by one of them

Ours was a "touring" car, not an enclosed sedan with windows, but it had side curtains for rainy weather. The windshield wiper was hand-operated. There was no heater. Flat tires were not unusual, so an effort was made to always carry an inner tube repair kit, an air pump, a jack, and other tools.

One learned to drive by doing it. There was no driver's education course in school. One Sunday as we were leaving my grandmother's house, my father asked if I wanted to drive. I got behind the wheel and, with minimum instruction, put the car into gear. I promptly ran into a tree. That was the end of my driving until one afternoon a few months later when I found the car keys, started the car, and took off by myself to visit a friend a mile or so away. When I had meetings at night at high school, my father always drove me to the meeting and waited until it was over to take me home. The first time I got to drive the car at night was for some event at the time of high school graduation.

Train, Bus, and Plane

Until we got our Ford, we made our annual trip to visit my father's sister and family in South Milwaukee by train. This was always an adventure for me. We took the Chicago, Milwaukee and St. Paul Railroad from Edgerton to Milwaukee, then the streetcar from Milwaukee to South Milwaukee. When I was in high school, I got to make this trip by myself.

By the time I was in high school, a Greyhound bus stopped in Edgerton about twice a day, each way. My first bus trip was in the fall of 1928 when my friend and I left for Madison to attend the University of Wisconsin. I am sure neither of my parents ever rode the bus.

Planes were such a novelty that if we heard one coming when we were working in the field, we would watch it from the time it appeared until it disappeared from sight. The first planes I saw were the single-engine biplanes used for stunt flying at the county fair. My first plane ride (and the only one until the late 1930s) was after graduation from high school in 1927 when three friends and I went to the Madison airport. At the time, I believe, the airport runway was made of dirt. A former World War I pilot made a business of taking up passengers. We paid five dollars for a five-minute flight. The plane was a single-engine, open cockpit biplane. The pilot sat in the front seat, the two passengers in the back. Two of my friends were the first to go. On their flight, the pilot looped-the-loop with them. The action when my friend and I went up included a side-slip before we landed; that was enough excitement for me.

The Telephone

The Walraths had a telephone in their part of the house. It was attached to the wall and had a mouthpiece into which one spoke. The receiver, held to the ear, was attached to a long cord. There was a small crank at the right side of the phone. This was a party line, serving ten or twelve families. Each family's phone had a distinctive ring, generated by the number of "long" cranks and the number of "short" cranks. The Walraths were reached by two long and three short cranks. Since this was a party line, everyone was free to listen to everyone else's calls if they so chose. It was understood that a long continuous call signaled an emergency, that help was needed. I never knew this to be put to use. To reach anyone not on the party line, one had to call the switchboard operator in Edgerton with a special crank signal. She would make the desired connection. Long-distance calls were rare. The phone line did not run beyond our place, so when the family on the adjoining farm needed to make an urgent call, the man would ask the Walraths if he could use their phone. One such occasion was when he tried to reach a doctor to come to the farm for the imminent birth of a child.

The Radio

Radio began to come into use in the 1920s. We never had one. Lack of electricity was one obstacle. Even if we had electricity, we might not have had a radio because of cost. The first time I heard a radio was when the family was visiting Mrs. Walrath's brother-in-law. He had just gotten this novelty, a radio. We took turns listening, using a headset. Later, he replaced the headset with a speaker, which was placed on the table beside the radio. My father was interested in heavyweight boxing championship fights. When these started to be broadcast by radio, we went a time or two to the home of an acquaintance who had a radio.

When I was in high school, I read about crystal set radios, which did not require electricity or batteries, and ordered one by mail. When it came, I put up a copper wire antenna from the henhouse near the orchard to the back porch of the house and ran the wire under a living room window to attach to my new crystal set. I put on the headset and manipulated the slender wire, attached to a knob, across the face of the crystal on the front part of the set. I never heard a sound. Finally, I lent the set to a high school classmate interested in radios. He told me that he did hear stations, but I never heard anything on my set.

Publications and Mail

We subscribed to the *Janesville Daily Gazette*—daily except Sunday. Our copy came by mail the day after publication. The Walraths took the weekly newspaper published in Edgerton but we rarely saw it. It was probably about 1920 when we started to receive the *Prairie Farmer*, a farm journal, regularly.

Letters and cards from my grandfather in Norway were especially welcome. My father corresponded with his parents until their deaths.

But years later, I learned that his father complained that the letters became "so English" that he had to have a translator. There was also some correspondence with my father's sister in South Milwaukee and with my mother's sister.

The mail also brought the large catalogs put out by Montgomery Ward and Sears Roebuck. I do not recall that anything was ordered from these catalogs. They became the usual source of toilet paper.

The mail carrier, always a man, came by horse and buggy or horse and cutter until he bought a car. In my time on the farm, there were only two carriers. The first married the daughter of the family next door to us and took over the farm. The second, after work, volunteered to help my father with tobacco harvest a time or two.

Other Contacts

There were fairly regular contacts with persons not relatives or friends. The "Watkins man," who sold spices, extracts, and the like, came with his horse and buggy about twice a year. He always came at noontime, had dinner with us, and had his horse fed. He always gave me a piece of gum. Of a different order were the stops once or twice a year by the man who was called the "shenney." He drove an underfed-looking horse pulling a small wagon. This man went farm to farm buying old iron and clean rags. I always looked for old iron such as horseshoes to sell for a few pennies.

9

Country School and High School

I completed grades one through eight at the country school, Cox School District No. 2, located about one mile from our farm. I started at the age of six in the spring of 1916, about two months before the end of the term. I have never forgotten my first day of school. The teacher put me at a desk on one side of the room near the front and gave me a reading book to look at. I started to turn the pages and, as I came to one page, called out, "See the rabbit run up the page." Immediately, the teacher came over to tell me that I couldn't talk out like that in school.

This was not my first experience at this school. When I was perhaps four, someone arranged to have me give a recitation at the Christmas program. My mother and I sat in the first row in front of the stage (a platform raised about twelve inches above floor level). As the other children did their parts, I was much more intrigued by the fireplace (make-believe) at the back of the stage than I was interested in the singing and performances of the children. When my name was called to do my recitation, I immediately got on the stage, walked to the back, and got on my knees trying to look up the "fireplace" chimney to see Santa Claus. That the audience burst into laughter did not concern me. My mother finally persuaded me to come back to the front of the stage to recite my piece. It was: "Here I stand just three feet high, hooray for Christmas and the Fourth of July!"

There was one other child, a boy, in the first grade. Before the school year ended, he died of diphtheria. The schoolhouse was closed to be fumigated, I was told. I did not understand what that meant.

The Schoolhouse and Grounds

The schoolhouse was a one-room, one-story building of yellow brick. It had a high ceiling, no basement. A few years after I started, an entryway of wood was added across the front. The schoolhouse had two doors at the front, only one of which was used. There were three windows on either side. Each corner at the back of the room had a built-in cupboard, one of which held chunks of wood for the wood-burning stove. A blackboard ran across the entire front of the room. The teacher's desk was in front. She faced five rows of desks for the students. The center row had double-desks. Every desk had an inkwell, and under the top there was storage space for books, paper, and pencils. Three kerosene lamps were attached to the wall on each side of the room; these were used only when there was an event at night. A small bookcase was in one corner in the front; its shelves were not filled. Two large pictures hung on one wall, one of George Washington, the other of Abraham Lincoln. When the entry was added, the children put their coats, rubbers, overshoes, and such there. The water pail, later a water fountain, was also in the entry, along with the drinking glass each child was supposed to have and a wash basin. I don't recall that the wash basin got much use.

Outside were a large woodshed and two outhouses, one for boys and one for girls. Those buildings were painted red. There was playground space in front of and on both sides of the school. At the back and along one side of the playground were a few shade trees. The only equipment was a homemade swing hung from the branch of a tree and a couple of baseball bats and balls. I do not recall that there was a flagpole.

An elected school board of three men, all farmers, hired the teacher and paid her salary from tax money collected for school purposes. In the fall, before school started, one of them mowed the grass and weeds that had grown on the grounds during the summer. They saw that a supply of wood was in the woodshed each fall for the stove. Before the Christmas program, they brought materials from their farms to build the stage for the program.

One of the school board members was the first in the neighborhood to get a tractor. The first day he used it in the field, our teacher took all of us, walking, to the farm to see the tractor at work.

Getting to School

There were not any school buses to transport children to our school (or to high school). Everyone, even the youngest, walked. When I was in the earlier grades, if the weather was stormy, my mother might come with umbrella or horse and buggy to take me home. Later, I persuaded my mother to buy rubber boots for me to wear on rainy days. On the way home, I always tested the depth of the pools of water along the roadside. Often, I found the water going over my boots. When I got home, my mother put oats in the boots to dry them out. Several times in the winter, I got frostbite on my cheeks, nose, and ears. One time when I was walking home, I met a big black man with a pack on his back. This was the first time I was close to a black person. He would fit in the category of what was called a tramp or hobo; why he was on this road is a mystery.

I was the only child in school who did not always walk. Starting when I was about in the fifth grade, I rode my pony, Beauty, to school. The first year, I left him in the barn of the nearest farm. After that, I tied him along the roadside near the school in warm weather and put him in the woodshed in cold weather. At the end of the school day, he was always anxious to get home. I had a metal pail for my lunch. If it rattled when I was getting on, he sometimes started off without me. I never caught up with him when he did this.

Teachers

One teacher taught all eight grades. There were no teachers' aides. During my eight grades, I had three different teachers, all young and unmarried. They were high school graduates with two years of what was called normal school. I had my first teacher for only about two months (I didn't start until near the end of the term). She moved to a different school the next year. I had the second teacher for the second, third, and fourth grades. She was the daughter of a farmer in the Edgerton area. The thing I most remember about this teacher was that on a wintry day, after school, she had a party at her parents' home for all of the children. A bobsled pulled by a team of horses and driven by one of the school board members took us there and took us home. Straw had been placed in the bottom of the wagon box mounted on the bobsled, and we had a lot of blankets to help keep us warm.

The third teacher, for my last four years, got room and board with one of the farm families whose children had completed school. This teacher was especially helpful for me. During the summer between the fifth and sixth grades, I broke my leg. I did not get back to school until the spring of the sixth grade year. Once a week, from the time school started in the fall until I went back to school in the spring, this teacher came to our house. She stayed overnight, gave me assignments for the next week, and checked what I had done during the past week. So I did not miss a grade. Every spring, a competition in spelling, arithmetic, and penmanship was held for students in the country schools in the Town of Fulton; this was part of a countywide program. My teacher entered me in this competition near the end of the sixth grade to give me the experience. The next year, I won the competition, and in my eighth grade year, I placed second.

When I was in first grade, the total school enrollment was about twenty-one or twenty-two pupils, the largest number of any time I was in school. Most of the time, there were twelve to fourteen. For a few of the early years, there were four in my grade, three girls and myself. Then two of the girls moved away, leaving two in my class for the rest of my country school days.

The Three Rs and Beyond

We learned grammar and reading; we diagrammed a lot of sentences on the blackboard. We learned arithmetic and did problems on the blackboard. We were taught the Palmer method of penmanship. The recitations were at the front of the room so all the children could hear what was being said. There were no electives during the eight years. I suppose the course of study was set by the county or state. Parents paid for the required books and for all the school supplies, such as paper, pencils, eraser, crayons, pen points, and pen holders.

Once a week, we had singing. Each child had a copy of a songbook. There was no musical accompaniment. I was never taught to read notes; we just sang. When the teacher asked what song we wanted to sing next, I would raise my hand and say, "Three Blind Mice," "Goodnight, Ladies," or "Old Black Joe" if we had not already had the song.

The third teacher gave us practice chairing a meeting and making and passing motions. I liked to preside. She also had us debate the pros and cons of a controversial topic that concerned the low prices farmers got compared with what they paid for things. The U.S. Congress passed legislation to encourage the organization of farmers' marketing cooperatives as a way to get better prices. In Wisconsin, there was a big drive to organize a tobacco marketing cooperative. Some of our neighbors joined; my father did not. At school I was on the team opposing the cooperative.

Special Activities and Programs

The most important program of the year put on for parents was the Christmas program. The children performed on the "stage" built for that purpose by school board members. A wire was stretched wall-to-wall for the curtain, which the teacher drew when the scene was being set for a performance. Children practiced the songs, the individual recitations, and the dialogues. The dialogues usually had two to four actors, all the older children. When parents and children arrived at the school on the evening of the program, the kerosene lamps had been lighted and a big, decorated Christmas tree with candles was in a corner at the front of the room. After the program, the candles were lighted and Santa Claus appeared with a pack on his back with presents for the children; the teacher assisted in distributing the presents. I have never forgotten one night when my parents and I walked home after the program. It was cold, the moon was full, and the star-filled sky made everything bright. The snow was crunchy underfoot and the snow-covered ground seemed to sparkle.

On Valentine's Day, we exchanged valentines. We drew names in advance to ensure that every child received a valentine.

We observed Arbor Day by using part of the school day to rake and clean up the school grounds and to plant a tree. One year, afterward, we all walked to the Indianford school, where we had a picnic together.

At the end of the school year, there was an afternoon picnic for the parents who could come. The picnic was in the woods at one of the farms. One year at the picnic, we had a special program with an Indian theme. Our mothers made our costumes.

At the end of the school year, it was customary to collect money from each family with children (about twenty-five cents per family) to buy a silver spoon for the teacher. Usually a child of the mother who made the purchase made the presentation to the teacher. I got to do this several times.

One activity was not a part of the school program, but was a money-raising event, probably sponsored by the Mothers Club to

The program for our school's end-of-year picnic had a Native American theme

support the hot lunch program. When the hot lunch program began to take hold, the Mothers Club decided this would be a good idea for our school. So during cold weather, the teacher, assisted by one of the older girls, would prepare a hot item—usually hot cocoa, soup, or rice—to supplement the lunch each child brought from home. Some years, a box social was held to support this program. The mothers, girls, and the teacher would decorate boxes or baskets filled with food for two persons. The box social was always held at the school at night. The boxes were auctioned off one by one by the same man who played Santa Claus. The winning bidder and the woman who contributed the box paired off to eat together. The teacher's box or basket was always one of those most finely decorated. When her box went up for bid, the men had some fun bidding up the price so the teacher's boyfriend would have to pay a lot, as much as five dollars, to get the box.

Student Tasks

In our school, the children had certain tasks. The school did not have a well, so water had to be brought each day from a farm about a quarter of a mile away. The teacher asked two of the older boys to take the pail and get the water. Eventually, we had a water fountain to hold the water but until then the pail was on a stand. Every child had his or her own glass or cup for drinking water, but these were all on the same stand with the pail or fountain so not all the children were too careful about getting their own cup.

When the heating stove was in use, the boys were expected to bring the chunks of wood from the woodshed and keep the cupboard for wood filled. The teacher started the fire in the morning and kept it going all day by adding chunks of wood. She also swept the floor after school. Mice sometimes made a home in the cupboard and chewed a hole at the bottom of the door to get in and out. One day, a mouse kept coming out of the cupboard into the schoolroom, so the teacher asked me to sit in the desk closest to the cupboard, with a stick of wood in my hand, and try to hit the mouse when it came out. I didn't succeed, but it was fun to have this assignment.

Another student task was to clean the blackboard and the erasers. At Thanksgiving time and Christmas, the blackboard was decorated with seasonal messages and scenes done with stencils and colored chalk. The older girls assisted the teacher with this task.

Lunchtime and Recess Activities

During good weather, as soon as it was lunchtime, the boys went to the back of the schoolhouse to eat their lunches. But before starting, they always compared lunches with each other and made trades if they preferred what another boy had. Desserts and fruit were most often traded.

The favorite outdoor games in good weather were baseball (work-up, not teams), hide and seek, tag, and a favorite called "anti-over." In this game, two teams were chosen, and they stood on opposite sides of the building. A ball was thrown over the roof of the school. The person who caught the ball would run around to the other side, along with the rest of the team, and try to tag someone on the other team. If tagged, the person had to join the tagger's team. Crack-the-whip was another outside game. All children could participate in these.

In winter, when there was snow, some of us brought our sleds to school so we could slide down the hill on the road that ran past the school. When there was a big snowdrift along the road opposite the school, we would tunnel in the snow and make caves. In late winter one year, rains had left a pond-like area on one side of the road between the school and the first farm in that direction. This "pond" froze over, and one noon the children asked if they could go there to slide on the ice. The teacher approved. When the children got to the pond, the girls all congregated in one place. This was "rubber ice," not solidly frozen ice. With the girls all in one spot, the ice broke and all of them fell into the water. They came back to school wet to their waists. The start of school had to be delayed until their clothes dried out as they stood around the stove.

Games inside the school building included "Fruit Basket Tips Over" and "Pin the Tail on the Donkey." We did not have any board games or card games.

Other Features of My Country School

The lack of an adequate library at our school was partly offset by the arrival about once a month of a big wooden box filled with books. When the box was opened, we all stood around it, pulling out books and choosing the ones we wanted to read first. I do not know where the box came from, but I suppose it was from a state educational agency. We did not have a traveling library in the county, as far as I know. The books were returned to the source each month.

Our annual "community service" project was selling Christmas seals to raise money to fight tuberculosis, a major health problem of that time. Seals were one cent each. The potential buyers were neighbors without children in school and our families. If I turned in one dollar for my sales, I had done well.

Once a year the county superintendent of schools visited our school. I do not know whether the teacher knew of the visit in advance. When it was time for school to start in the morning or after recess and lunch, the teacher would come outside and ring a small handbell. I never had homework when I was in country school. I have no recollection of the pupils saying the Pledge of Allegiance; if we did, it did not make a lasting impression. I never heard mention of school prayer in or out of school. During my time in Cox School

District No. 2, I never knew a teacher to have a discipline problem with any student.

High School

Most families in the neighborhood, but not all, sent their children to high school. This was not a matter for discussion in my family. At a Sunday dinner at our place, with relatives, my mother stated that I would be going to high school. The German-born wife of one of my uncles immediately said, "He must be going to be a minister." This, apparently, was the only reason she could think of for going beyond the eighth grade.

The high school in Edgerton was five miles away. There was no bus service. All children in the country had to provide their own transportation. My mother arranged for me to ride with a boy who was a high school senior. We paid him one dollar per week. Each morning, I had to walk about one and a half miles to the home of another boy who was to be picked up. Our other passengers were the driver's sister, also just starting high school, and another girl who was picked up at her home. When we came home after school, I was let out at the country school and walked the rest of the way home. After the first year, I rode with the boy who lived on the farm where I was picked up the first year. Again, I walked to his house in the morning and from my country school in the afternoon. We rode in a Ford Model T touring car. Icy roads were not uncommon in the winter. One morning we were on our way to school, going down a hill with a gentle slope but ice covered. The car started to slide to the side of the road. The driver could not control it. When the car came to the side of the road, it tipped over on its top, throwing me through the cloth-like top. Neither I, the driver, nor the other two passengers were injured. We uprighted the car and continued on our way. That evening, I casually told my mother what had happened. The experience gave me a lifelong fear of driving on ice.

On another occasion, when I was let out at the country school, there had been a lot of snow during the day and it was snowing heavily. I reached one point in the road where I knew a deep drift lay ahead, difficult to get through. I decided to go across a field to avoid the drift, but the snow on the field was deep, and I became very tired. I sank down into the snow to rest. This felt good, but I knew it could be fatal to stay there in the cold. Finally, I summoned up enough strength to get up and go on. Before long, I could see the welcome sight of the lights at our place.

If I had a meeting or a party at school at night and my father did not want to take me and wait for me, it was understood that I could stay overnight with Mrs. Walrath's sister and her husband. The same held for nights when there was a bad snowstorm. This couple rented a house in a poorer part of town. He worked at the highway trailer manufacturing plant. There seemed to be fairly frequent job layoffs, some of them prolonged. More than once when I went to stay over-night and it was suppertime, I would be told, "We don't have much to eat." Supper would be fried potatoes, bread, and coffee. Breakfast was the same. Two or three times after school parties, I stayed over-night with a classmate who lived in town.

Introduction to High School

The high school was a big change for a farm boy from a one-teacher school with twelve or fourteen students. The red brick building had separate entrances for boys and girls; this meant that before school and at noon, the boys congregated on their side and the girls on their side. The school superintendent's office was on the first floor near the entrance on the boys' side. A large room called the assembly, where every student had an assigned desk, was on the second floor. It had three entrances, two at the front and one at one side. Part of the assembly was over the gymnasium used for basketball, physical education, school parties, and special events such as the science fair. If the students in the assembly moved in unison, the part of the assembly floor over the gym would move up and down.

On the first day, I found the room for three of my classes, but it was not until the third day that I finally located my English class. I thought I probably had to go down one of the two front entrances to the assembly, but was hesitant to ask anyone. At the beginning of each school day with all students, freshmen through seniors, in the assembly the superintendent would make any announcements needed for that day. The student in the back desk in each row of desks would check attendance. At noon, students were permitted to go off the school grounds but not to any of the pool halls in town. I knew, without being told, that my parents would not approve of my going to a pool hall, which they would consider a place where the "less desirable" young men gathered and loitered. When students were not in class, they returned to their desk in the assembly to study. There was a small library off the assembly room for use. During these study hours, a teacher was always on duty to watch for misconduct. At the end of the school day, all students were back in the assembly to hear announcements, including the names teachers had placed

The high school I attended in Edgerton, 1923–27 (Wisconsin Historical Society, WHi-30869)

on the "conduct list." Those listed had to stay after school for half an hour.

My ride home seldom got started soon after school. The girls always seemed to have something to do so they did not appear at the designated departure point until five o'clock or later. Consequently, after school, I almost always went to the public library, directly in back of the high school, where I browsed among the books and magazines. Often by the time I got home, especially in the winter when it was always dark, my family was finished with supper.

The home economics department operated a noontime cafeteria with low-cost hot and cold items for students and teachers. I always carried my lunch, but my mother gave me ten cents a day to get something at the cafeteria.

There were about seventy-five students in my freshman class. In the beginning, I knew only two of them, besides those I first knew when we rode to school together: my girl classmate from country school and a girl whose family visited the Walraths. The total high school enrollment was probably about two hundred, perhaps less. In my senior year, there were eighteen faculty members, two men and sixteen women. One man taught manual training, the other coached all boys' sports. Most of the women teachers seemed to fit one of two groups. The teachers in one group were young, recently out of college, and unmarried; those in the other group were "career" teachers, unmarried and middle aged or older.

Courses and Teachers

Students worked out their course schedules with the help of the superintendent or someone in his office. There were no guidance counselors. There were few electives; all students took about the same set of courses over the four years. I wished the high school offered vocational agriculture, but it did not. As an entering freshman, I had to choose one elective from among manual training, home economics, French, or Latin. I chose manual training, so I had to also take it in the second year. In this school, boys did not take French or Latin. As for me, a farm boy who had no idea that he would be going to college, French and Latin seemed to be of little value. The required courses for freshmen were algebra, English, and science. Physical education was also required. Before I graduated, I had four years of

English, three years of math, and three years of history. Other courses included physics (we had to choose between chemistry and physics), economics, sociology, and speech.

When I finally found my freshman English class, I discovered it was about literature, starting with *Silas Marner*. I had the same teacher for sophomore and junior English. One year we studied poetry. The other year emphasized writing. I still remember one essay I wrote: "The Common Meal as a Socializer." That same course gave considerable attention to parliamentary procedure; I liked it when something came up, so I could stand up and say, "I rise to a point of order." The senior English class was on Shakespeare. The teacher also had some administrative responsibility at the elementary school across the street. When she got a call in the middle of class to go to the elementary school, she would often ask me to take over the class. Fellow students accepted this and the class went on.

For geometry, advanced mathematics, and American history; I had an excellent teacher who had a way of making the subjects interesting. The teacher for the ancient history class would let the students divert the discussion to topics far from ancient history. During one class session, the discussion turned to an argument among students as to whether Red Grange, a football star at the University of Illinois, should have turned professional. The only class I did not really like was physics, because the teacher, I felt, had wrongly accused me of helping another student during class. The course in manual training gave me something to remember. In the second year, a classmate and I got into a mock duel with wood chisels. The problem was that his chisel went into my cheek and left me with a small scar.

Occasionally, an assembly would be called to hear a speaker. The only special assembly I remember was when Calvin Coolidge was president. Radios were still new, a novelty, at the time. When the superintendent learned that the president was going to address the nation by radio (apparently a "first"), he called the assembly so we could all be aware of this new way of communicating.

My sociology teacher selected me to represent our school at a district current events contest for high schools in several counties. I received a medal for third place.

Activities in High School

After my first year, I joined some organizations. When a Hi-Y Club was started in my sophomore year, I joined. When I was a senior, I tried out for the Thespians, which put on plays, and was selected. The biggest disappointment of my high school career was getting mumps just before the tryouts for the major production of the year. When the director of the school band decided to start a drum and bugle corps, I signed up to play a drum. Shortly after I became involved, I took my drum home and started to practice after my father was already in bed. My practice was promptly terminated, and that was the end of my participation in any musical organization. While I was in high school, the Masonic lodge decided to organize a DeMolay chapter. Along with several of my classmates, I joined. The ritual did not appeal to me, interest among my peers proved to be low, and, in about a year, the chapter became inactive.

When I started high school, I was still protective of the leg I had broken when I was ten years old. I was a senior before I was permitted to go out for football. I weighed 135 pounds at the time; the coach had me in the line at tackle. The team had nine games that year and won seven. I got to go with the team on all of its out-of-town trips, in cars driven by faculty or players. But I played in only one game, when the coach sent me in when the game was hopelessly lost.

I went out for track when I was a junior. The school did not have a track. That spring, interested students, under the supervision of the coach, built a track in back of the high school. In my senior year, I won my letter running the mile. I also ran in the mile relay in a district meet for schools from several counties and placed. At the athletic awards banquet in my senior year, the coach asked me to speak for the track team. I think that was the proudest moment of my high school career.

Every fall, each class elected officers for the year—a president, vice president, secretary, and treasurer. In my sophomore year, I was secretary. The vote for class president in my class always seemed to be along gender lines. My senior class had twenty-five girls and fifteen boys. That year, the girl who was my country school classmate was nominated for president, and so was I. She won. I was elected vice president.

Our senior class trip to Madison was a one-day affair. We went in cars driven by faculty and students. The first stop was at the Wisconsin Hospital for the Insane. The visit there made a lasting impression. We saw violent patients confined in tubs and with other restraints. We were told the cause of some of the cases was venereal diseases. Our second stop was at the capitol building, where we were given a tour. I was impressed by the grandeur of the interior.

Our class yearbook was called *The Crimson*. I was the athletics editor. It featured two stories written by seniors. One of them was mine: "The Midnight Visitor," my first publication and the only piece of fiction I have ever had published. *The Crimson* had a picture of each senior, a record of activities and honors, and, at the bottom, a statement about each student. The one for me read, "He seeks to know and gets what he goes after."

Awards

Looking back, I have never had any doubt that the teachers in my one-room country school prepared me for the academic side of the high school I attended. At least, I fared well in my high school's awards for scholarship. The same was true of my country school classmate.

Two boys and two girls were selected from each class to be in the Achievement Group. I was selected each of my four years. In my senior year, I was made a member of the National Honor Society and of the Iron Cross, a new organization at the time, by vote of faculty and students. I was one of the six boys and six girls elected to the Service Organization by student vote. And I was made a member of the National Athletic Scholarship Society, a new organization.

Graduation and After

Commencement exercises on June 1 and June 2 were held in the high school auditorium. We did not wear caps and gowns. The speaker on the first evening was a faculty member from Beloit College. Shortly before our graduation, Charles Lindbergh had made his historic solo

My high school graduation photo, 1927

flight in the *Spirit of St. Louis* across the Atlantic. Lindbergh had been a student at the University of Wisconsin, giving his feat a special significance for us. The speaker used Lindbergh's achievement as the theme for his remarks. On the second evening, when the diplomas were given out, four students, including my country school classmate, received special awards. My part in the commencement program was to present the class gift, a desk, to the teacher who taught the senior English class.

Of the graduating class of forty, not more than half went to college or for special training. The school superintendent encouraged me to apply to the University of Wisconsin, which was to start an experimental college the following fall. For the first two years, the students would live in the same dormitory and study the Great Books. My interest was in the College of Agriculture, so I did not apply for this new university program. My plan was to stay out of school for a year, on the farm, and then go to the College of Agriculture. In the summer of 1928, I learned that the College of Agriculture was offering five $100 scholarships to entering freshmen. One summer evening, I sat down at the kitchen table with a kerosene-lit lamp and wrote my application. I was one of the five to receive this award.

In September, my good friend, who had also stayed out of school for a year, and I decided to go to Madison a week early, find a room, and look for work. I had five hundred dollars in savings. When our mothers saw us off on the bus in Edgerton, my friend and I said we would be home for Thanksgiving. We found a room right away, close to the campus, for which we each paid three dollars a week. At the end of that first week, not having found a job, we decided to take the bus to Edgerton. Our parents were surprised to see us that Saturday night.

At the end of the first semester, my grades earned me a second $100 scholarship. The faculty adviser I was assigned to, a professor of agricultural journalism, was my adviser and mentor for the next five years. The required English course was devoted solely to various forms of writing. One of my compositions was based on a field trip that my animal husbandry class had taken to the big meat packing plant in Madison. Normally, the instructor returned our papers to us to keep after he had commented on and graded them. My vivid account of what I had seen in the packing plant, including a description of a rabbi's ritual at the slaughter of an animal so that it would be kosher, so intrigued the instructor that, after having me read my work to the class, he kept it.

My friend and I each mailed our laundry home regularly in a "laundry box." We looked forward to the return of our laundered clothes because our mothers always included food, such as cookies and fruit.

When my friend went on a field trip with his geology class, he spotted two young owls displaced from their nest. After the trip, he returned to the spot and brought the two young owls back to our room. He put them in a box, put the box in our closet, and fed and watered them every day until they were fully grown and could no longer be kept in the closet. Our landlady would have been much surprised and displeased had she found out about the owls in our closet.

I had gone to college with the idea of being a farmer. That first year began to make me aware of the alternative possibilities, such as in agricultural journalism. I ended up with my major in that field.

The freshman who received the highest grades for the year had his name (I don't think there were any girls in our class) inscribed on a big Alpha Zeta cup, which was kept on display in the entrance area to Agriculture Hall. I ended the year in a three-way tie for this honor.

Early in the fall, I listed my name with the university's student employment office. I was referred to two jobs: waiter at a sorority during "rushing," and busboy at a hotel restaurant during a football weekend. I didn't feel comfortable with either of these. Then, through a high school acquaintance, I got a job peeling potatoes for my meals at a restaurant with a fancy dining room, although the basement, where I peeled three bushels of potatoes every afternoon, was dark, damp, and usually dirty.

At the end of the first year, I went home to work on the farm for the summer. My father had offered to pay me seventy-five dollars a month, well above the going rate for a hired man. After that summer, my life and work on our farm were limited to weekend visits and short vacations.

10

Health and Medical Care

When I was young, doctors made house calls in the country. Home remedies were the rule for colds and chest congestion. Immunization and vaccination of young children were not routine. One day in high school, all the students were vaccinated for smallpox.

I never knew my father or mother to go to a doctor's office or have one come to our house for them. I had a doctor three times for my left leg. When I was still crawling, I somehow fell over the rocker of a rocking chair and dislocated my leg. But this was not recognized until I could not walk when it was time; I just dragged my leg. Finally, I was taken to a specialist in Chicago who corrected the problem. His fee was one hundred dollars. When I was old enough to realize what the fee was, I could not believe it. I knew it was a lot of money for my parents at the time.

When I was six years old, on a Monday washday, my mother had put a bunch of green onions on the porch for me to clean. Instead, I started to go off the porch and slipped on the green onion tops. I fell the three steps to the brick surface and broke my leg. The doctor was called. He arrived the next day, by horse and buggy, accompanied by another doctor. They placed me on the kitchen table and set my leg. The doctor went out to the woodshed, where he found some boards to make a splint for my leg. A bed was set up in the living room for me. The next step was for the doctor to make a weight by putting sand into a pail that had been used for syrup or something similar. This pail of sand was attached to my leg with a pulley device made right there.

When I was ten, I broke my leg for a second time. I had been watching our cows along the road one morning in early summer, riding my pony. For some reason, the cows started to leave and I started after them with my pony. The saddle slipped, and I fell to the road. I pulled myself to the side of the road. Soon a neighbor came along in his car and saw me. I asked him to go get my father. He came back with my father, and we went to the house. The next thing I knew, I was lying on the ironing board, which had been placed across the back seat of the neighbor's car. I was taken to the office of three doctors who had been doctors in World War I. They had a new device in their office, an X-ray machine. They x-rayed my leg and set it. This time I was taken to the home of Mrs. Walrath's sister in town, where a bed was set up for me. I stayed there until it was decided my leg had healed sufficiently to go home. I was on crutches for a long time. That fall I was not ready to go back to school.

When I got a cold in my chest, before I started country school, my mother had two treatments. One was to put goose grease on my chest; the other was an onion poultice. She would fry a lot of onions on the kitchen stove and put them in a cloth bag. The bag was placed over my chest and held in place with safety pins pinned to my nightgown. I would have to wear this poultice all night. One of our elderly male neighbors swore by skunk grease as the best treatment for a chest cold.

If I needed a laxative when I was young, I was given either castor oil or Epsom salts. Both tasted terrible. I was always glad when slices of orange were available to eat afterward.

I was aware of the influenza epidemic of 1918 but at the time did not comprehend how serious it was. The man for whom my father worked as a hired man died from the flu. My father got the flu. I saw him wrapped in blankets and sitting in a rocking chair in our living room, with his feet in a basin of warm water, and I heard the adults talk about his high fever. But he recovered. I remember times when he came home from the field at the end of a day of spring's work complaining of a fever. I do not think he ever lost time from work because of these fevers.

Tuberculosis was an important public health problem. For this reason, all farmers were required to have their cattle tested; the ones found to have tuberculosis were taken away. A middle-aged man who worked as a hired man for one of our neighbors got tuberculosis, or consumption, as it was referred to in humans. As was customary, this man was sent to a tuberculosis sanatorium for care. He did not recover.

Mr. Walrath was subject to attacks of asthma. His remedy was what looked like ground-up leaves of some kind, which he took from a small can he had purchased, I suppose, at a drugstore. He poured this substance on the metal cover of the can, lit the material, and inhaled the smoke.

In 1922, Mr. Walrath had abdominal pain and was taken to the nearest major hospital, in Janesville. I was taken to visit him. The hospital was staffed by black-garbed nuns who seemed to move silently about. I felt very uncomfortable in the situation. Mr. Walrath was operated on for appendicitis, developed an infection, and died. Antibiotics were unheard of at the time.

My father never went to a dentist or needed to, as far as I knew. But my mother started having dental problems before she was married and continued to need fillings. When I was in country school, I began to get cavities but I refused my mother's efforts to get me to the dentist. Finally, when some teeth began to hurt, I gave in. Later, I regretted that I had not started dental care sooner.

A number of middle-aged and older men in the neighborhood had "ruptures," that is, damaged hernias, as a result of the heavy lifting that some tasks on the farm required. All of these men wore a truss, a device to reduce a hernia by pressure. None had surgery for their hernias.

11

Playtime, Pets, and Projects

I was an only child. There were no children close to my age on nearby farms. I did not get to see or play with children until I went to country school at age six. At a very young age, I sometimes created imaginary playmates, especially a sister. Outside, I could play with the house cats. We had a dog, Ted, but he did not mean a lot to me. Inside the house, I played with toys received at Christmas.

On Christmas Eve, I hung up my stocking on a wall in the living room because we did not have a fireplace. When I got up on Christmas morning, the stocking held an orange, some English walnuts, and hard candy, and a decorated Christmas tree had gifts under it. One Christmas Eve after I had been put to bed, I woke up, thought I heard a noise, peeked out, and saw my parents putting up the tree. I did not let on that I had seen them. During those early years, I remember getting a metal battleship that could be rolled along, small train cars of metal, a paper circus set to assemble, and coloring books. One windup toy was called the Alabama Coon Jigger. When wound up, the black-faced figure danced on a metal platform. It apparently did not occur to anyone at that time that this was a derogatory term. As I got a little older, I asked for a Daisy BB gun. After two or three years of asking with no results, I gave up on this.

As I grew old enough to no longer be restricted to one area around the house and the barn, I found that I had a 160-acre playground to explore and roam at will. I found wildlife—rabbits, squirrels, woodchucks, gophers, and chipmunks. The chipmunks liked to live close to a secluded rail fence. Once I saw a mother skunk walking along a fenceline with six or seven young skunks following in a single file, all with tails erect. One pasture had a marshy area with frogs. In another pasture was a small pond below surrounding hills; here I sometimes surprised two or three wild ducks or other waterfowl. This same pond always had an abundance of tadpoles in the spring.

My "playground" had a variety of birds. I liked to watch the hawks circling gracefully overhead, looking for prey on the ground. There were bluebirds with nests in wood fenceposts. Woodpeckers and sapsuckers made holes in the trees for their nests. One day I found a big hole in an apple tree trunk. When I put my hand inside, something nipped my finger; apparently young sapsuckers were there waiting for food. There were killdeer, bobolinks, blackbirds, crows, and other birds.

In the wooded pasture and along the fencerows, I found different kinds of trees. Most were oaks providing acorns. A few tall hickory trees yielded nuts every fall. Out of place were the two or three catalpa trees with their long pods; these may have been planted. Chokecherries along the fencelines produced large quantities of fruit for the birds. In the spring, I found wildflowers to pick—buttercups, violets, and the rare shooting stars. In season were wild black raspberries, asparagus, and a few gooseberries.

My mother, my pony, and me

When I was seven or eight, and after my pony, Beauty, had been trained, I learned to ride him. At first I rode bareback; later I had an English saddle. I was also given a two-wheeled cart with harness. With the cart it was easy to take my fishing equipment and go to Indianford to fish by myself. And a few times I ventured to drive as far as Edgerton. Next, I converted an old buggy into a light, four-wheeled wagon that Beauty could pull. After corn had been cut with the binder in the fall, we could go into the field and pick up a load of ears that had been

My father and Jack, on the back porch of the house

knocked off and take the load to feed the hogs. We could go to the field and get a load of ripe pumpkins to feed the cows.

My dog, Jack, became my closest companion from the time I was given him, when he was about six weeks old and I was about ten years old. We would walk the woods and fields together. We went woodchuck hunting. When we found one and it ran up a tree, I would knock it down and Jack would take care of it. I found a limb, shaped something like the rifle I never got and about the right length. I would take this and say to Jack, "Let's go rabbit hunting." Away we would go. When he scared up rabbits, I would go "bang, bang" with my gun as he chased after them. We never caught one. Sometimes our hunt would take us onto parts of other farms that were hilly and not in sight of the owner's house. On one spring day when the fragrance of blossoming fruit trees filled the air, I sat in my red wagon with Jack by my side. I looked up into the beautiful changing cloud formations. I had heard the name God, and as I looked at the clouds, I imagined that I might be seeing the changing faces of God in the clouds.

My Special Projects

About the time I was old enough to go to school, I came up with special projects or ideas for such projects. I started a weekly newspaper, a few pages handwritten. This lasted two or three issues. I started a bank. I had one depositor, an uncle who put in a nickel. The bank closed. When I learned a little about parliamentary procedure, I organized a club whose members were Jack, Beauty, one cat, and myself. We held meetings outside the barn and made, debated, and passed motions. We decided to have a garden where each member had an area two or three feet square. Each member planted something different, like a tobacco plant, a hill of corn, beans, or peas. We did this a couple of years. About the time I was ten, I wanted a piece of land in the worst way. I imagined the little house and the little barn I would build on it, a place where I could live by myself. I knew exactly where the land was that I wanted for my farm. One day when Mr. Walrath invited me to go for a ride with him in his car, I got up my courage to ask if he would sell me an acre of land. I am sure the question took him by surprise. He was noncommittal but I knew I was not going to get the acre I dreamed about.

Another project was to build a lean-to in the woods where I might sleep overnight. I found a site high on a hill in the woods, a site with a view. Two trees were spaced just the right distance apart and had crotches into which I placed a strong branch. I nailed this to the trees. Then I collected or cut limbs the right length to cover one side of the lean-to. The project did not get finished. But one time when I came home from college, I found that my father had cut these trees for firewood. When they were being sawed into chunks, the buzz saw ran into one of the nails I had driven into the trees. The saw was damaged.

Then I got an idea for building an airplane. I would take my red wagon, add wings, and make a propeller out of a part of a discarded washing machine. I figured that by starting at the top of the hill where my lean-to was, I could turn the propeller fast enough that by the time the wagon got to the bottom of the hill, we would be in the air. It is probably fortunate that I did not get far enough on my project to put my idea into practice.

Another project was a science club. The shipping crate for an upright piano had been brought to the farm by friends of the Walraths. I put a door on it, built shelves inside, and painted Science Club on the outside. This became the place to display the interesting stones I found, the large pieces of fungus found growing on trees, bird nests, and other items that interested me. I liked to show my science club to my friends when they came to see me.

I read in a magazine about trapping, trap lines, and selling furs. I bought half a dozen traps. In winter, I would find holes dug by woodchucks and skunks along the fencelines that looked as though they were being used. I would set my traps at the entrance of these holes. In the morning before going to school, I would take my make-believe gun and a gunnysack and, with Jack, check the traps. Sometimes I would find a rabbit, which I would bring home, skin, clean, and give to my mother so we could have fried rabbit. The first time I caught a skunk I did not know how to skin it and prepare the pelt so it could be sold. I put the dead skunk in a gunnysack and, riding Beauty, dragged the skunk in the sack to an elderly man a mile away who knew all about such things. He showed me how to skin a skunk properly. He made a stretcher out of a shingle, put the pelt over it, and cleaned the pelt so it was ready to be dried. When it was dry, I took the pelt to a merchant to sell. I got $1.25 for this one. The next time I caught a skunk, I knew what to do. Once I caught an ermine, a weasel turned white in the winter. I received $0.25 for that pelt.

Another project was my membership in the 4-H Club for four years. My interest in this started when I went to a meeting with my parents that had been called to promote 4-H Club work. I persuaded my father to let me join the calf club. In the spring, I selected a heifer calf to care for. As required, I recorded the amounts she was fed and what she weighed each month. I groomed and trained her how to stand and how to walk when she was being judged at the fair. The county fair lasted about three days. The 4-H Club calves were kept in a large tent. Many club members stayed all night with their calves. The first year, my parents thought I was too young to do this and arranged for me to stay at night with friends of the Walraths. Late each afternoon, I would go by streetcar to their friends' house. It was while staying there that I got to use a bathtub for the first time. For the next three years, I got to stay with my calf at night. One year, my calf was selected to go to the Wisconsin State Fair. The adult 4-H leader rented a boxcar to take the chosen calves, pigs, and sheep to the fair. He built a deck over the animals in one part of the boxcar and put straw on the deck. A few club members, including me, got to make the overnight trip, sleeping on the deck. The day of the judging was always a day of special activity. The calf had to be bathed and groomed and its hooves polished. My calf always won a ribbon but never a blue one (given for first place).

I liked to read. I started with books written for boys my age. Sometimes, when I was not in school and before I was working regularly in the summer, I would sit in the rocking chair by a window in the kitchen and read and read. One time, my mother said, "Why don't you go out and play?" When I got older, I had free access to Mrs. Walrath's library. My favorite books were by Zane Grey, such as *Riders of the Purple Sage.*

Activities with Family and Other Adults

I don't remember ever being read to. But I do recall winter evenings when my parents, other adults present, and I would sit around the kitchen table playing cards—Old Maid, Smear, and Seven-Up. Other nights we might help my mother pick the nutmeats out of the hickory nuts and black walnuts. Sometimes in the evening we had popcorn (home grown), popped in a wire basket on top of the kitchen stove. The basket had to be moved constantly so the kernels would not scorch. Once in a great while, the men would tell ghost stories and my father would tell about trolls (elves) in Norway, which were mischievous and could be trouble-makers, for example, letting the horses out of the barn. At these times, I would sit on the floor close to my mother. When Mrs. Walrath replaced her small table-model Victrola with an upright model in a beautiful cabinet, she would invite us in to listen to music. It was an achievement when I learned to change the records.

Sometimes my father would entertain us with his "feats of skill." One was lifting a kitchen chair by the rung with one hand from a kneeling position. Another was riding a jug. This meant sitting astride an earthenware jug, which once held a gallon of vinegar, and trying to avoid falling off as the jug rolled. Another was to get on the floor, legs outstretched, one arm behind his back and the other holding him up, and lowering himself to pick a handkerchief off the floor with his teeth.

When my parents went visiting or to parties, they took me with them. I did not get to stay home by myself until I was partway through high school. Nearly all the visiting with other families was with relatives. The exceptions were when we went to visit the family where my parents had worked before they were married and the family for whom they raised tobacco the first year they were married. The visits to my aunt and her family in South Milwaukee were always special. The first I remember was at Christmastime. My parents and

I slept on the floor. On Christmas Eve, my aunt had us all hold hands and dance around the lighted Christmas tree. I remember going to homes for parties. One of these was an oyster stew supper. At another, a daughter who was studying to be a music teacher sang some numbers. Most often, parties were at the town hall. There might be dancing or card playing or a program put on by the children. These parties were always in the winter months. We went by team and bobsled; the horses were covered with a horse blanket to keep them warm. At the end of the evening, the younger children, tired out, could be found asleep lying on coats around the big stove that heated the place.

The most exciting family vacation was a trip to the Wisconsin Dells, north of Madison, after we had our Model T. The trip and the boat tour were uneventful but it was late afternoon before we started for home. It started to rain and got dark. The highway was unpaved and the road got very muddy. A rear tire came off in the mud. In the dark, my father could not find the tire. We were stranded. So we went to a nearby farmhouse. The family gave us supper, took us in for the night, and gave us breakfast. In daylight, the lost tire was found and put back on the wheel rim, and we went on our way home.

When I was in country school, the Walraths would sometimes stop by after school and take me with them to a church supper, especially the ones when lutefisk was being served. They also sometimes took me with them to visit their friends. On summer evenings, Mr. Walrath sometimes asked me if I would like to "take a ride around the block" in his car.

On one memorable trip, my father invited me to go with him to a mill that specialized in grinding wheat into flour. We set out with team and wagon. It seemed as if it took two or three hours to get to the mill, located on a stream at a place I had never been to before. While our wheat was being ground, we ate the lunch my mother had sent with us. When the flour was ready, we headed back home, arriving in late afternoon.

Eating out at restaurants was not a part of my growing-up experience. The first time I ate in a restaurant was when Mrs. Walrath invited us to go to a Chinese restaurant in Janesville. The food was unfamiliar, the restaurant was heavily curtained and dark, and the staff were all Chinese—people I had never seen before. We went back there again a time or two. While it was an "experience," I did not really enjoy it.

When I was no more than five or six years old, I had one of my best experiences with adults. One day, Porter asked if I would like to go fishing with him. My mother gave permission. Porter and I dug worms in the place behind the log cabin where they could always be found. We set off down the road with cane poles, the worms, and a pail to put the fish in. We went to the neighboring farm where in the pasture was a body of water almost too large to be called a pond, but not quite large enough to be called a lake. When we arrived, we went to a spot where we could sit on a concrete structure. Porter put a bobber and hook on the line and showed me how to put the bait on the hook, how to toss out the line, and how to watch the bobber to see if there was a bite. We soon began to catch panfish and that was my start at being a committed fisherman. I went back there with

Porter many times. There were bullheads in different parts of the pond. Porter showed me how to put a hook and weight on a throw line and throw the line out, without a bobber, and watch the line for a bite.

When I was older, Mr. Walrath took me with him to Indianford where there was a dam on Rock River. On one side of the dam he stood on the concrete structure and fished with metal rod, reel, and artificial lures. I watched him catch large pike in the somewhat turbulent water below the dam. When I was older, I hitched Beauty to the cart, took my fishing equipment, and fished at Indianford dam on the opposite end from where I went with Mr. Walrath. I was going after the panfish with worms. After Mr. Walrath's death, Mrs. Walrath gave me his rods, reels, lures, and big minnow bucket; these got years of use.

When I was to be sixteen, Mrs. Walrath decided there should be a birthday party for me. About a dozen boys and girls, classmates, were invited. The kitchen was cleared for the occasion, which was in the evening. All we did was stand around, eat refreshments, and talk, and I opened my presents. It was not a party I wanted, but I had no choice.

Activities with My Peers

I was probably halfway through country school when somehow I became acquainted with a boy my own age who went to another country school and lived on a farm about a mile and a half away. He also had a pony. We visited each other frequently, eating dinner at each other's house with no advance arrangements. Sometimes I walked across the back part of the intervening farm to get to my friend's place. We had cookouts in his woods. We found that an old abandoned house in a secluded part of his farm had piles of old books and magazines. We liked to look through these, hoping to find something to keep. Another boy at my school also had a pony and two others shared a horse to ride. At times, we would all gather at my place and play cowboys and Indians, on pony and horse, in one of our pastures. And when riding together on the road, we would decide to race; Beauty was usually the fastest.

I had classmates from three families with whom I also visited, riding Beauty. I especially liked going to one, the most distant, because the mother always had angel food cake, which I thought was the best I ever had.

In high school, I developed friendships with three other boys that lasted a lifetime. Only one of us was permitted to drive a car, so he provided the transportation for whatever we did together, including visiting and eating at each other's homes. A couple of times, we went duck and goose hunting on Lake Koshkonong. This meant staying overnight with one of the friends, getting up early to be at the lake before daylight and well hidden so we would be ready when the waterfowl began to fly. I used the shotgun kept in the closet off the living room in my house. We had some success.

Our high school did not have a swimming pool. One night, the friend who drove took us to a creek he knew about and we all went swimming in a place I knew nothing about. When a lodge was built near Indianford with an outdoor swimming pool that could be used for a fee, we went there a couple of times.

Holidays and Special Events

On Thanksgiving, Christmas, New Year's, and Easter, my mother always had an especially good dinner. On Easter morning, when I was young, I would try to get up early enough to see the Easter bunny; I never quite succeeded. But at the table, I would find an Easter basket with small fluffy yellow chicks, candy Easter eggs, and maybe a chocolate bunny. At Halloween, at suppertime, there might be a jack-o-lantern with lighted candles and candy corn.

On Memorial Day, a parade was held in Edgerton. The parade always had at least one open touring car with Civil War veterans in their uniforms. On July 4, I always looked forward to going to the village where my grandmother lived because of the celebration—games for children, tug of war for the men in the morning, and a baseball game in the afternoon. We did not go anywhere to see fireworks, but it was the custom that we had fireworks in our backyard on the Fourth. I think this started when I was old enough to be given one dollar to buy fireworks. We had small and large firecrackers, sparklers, and—best of all—Roman candles, which went up in the air quite a distance.

That the family would go to the county fair in Janesville for one day each year was a "given." We would go in the morning and look at the livestock and other exhibits. At noon, we would eat the lunch my mother had brought. In the afternoon, we would buy tickets for a seat in the grandstand. There we watched the harness races (trotters and pacers); my father was an enthusiastic watcher of the races and seemed to know if a horse was descended from some well-known racehorse. There was always entertainment on the platform in front of the grandstand, such as acrobats and trapeze artists. We never got to watch the evening fireworks because we had to get home for the evening chores.

Ringling Brothers Circus came to Janesville for a day each year, setting up its tents on the fairgrounds. My mother took me to an afternoon performance two or three times. The circus traveled by train. In the morning, the animals and circus wagons were paraded through downtown Janesville from the train to the fairgrounds. We always watched the parade. At the performance, the clowns were always of special interest, but I enjoyed watching all the acts.

12

Other Memories
of My Life on the Farm

Weather and Storms

Weather was always a matter of concern on the farm, especially during the spring to fall seasons. If there was not enough rain, crops would not grow well and pastures would dry up. With too much rain, planting could not be done on time or corn could not be cultivated to keep ahead of the weeds. Wind with rain could "lodge" the grain at harvest time so the stalks were not upright for cutting. Too much rain after the hay had been mowed but not brought to the barn could lower the quality of the hay.

Some neighbors had lightning rods on their barn and house; we did not. One summer day, there was a bad storm and lightning hit a tall elm tree at the corner of the log house. We had all been in the kitchen during the storm. With the lightning strike, we all dashed out to see bluish smoke, acrid-smelling. The elm tree had been split. A moment after the strike, my dog, Jack, who had been in the log house, came outside, howling, at full speed.

Homemade Clothes

My mother put her sewing machine to good use. She made most of her own clothes. When I was about four or five years old, she made two items for me that I was not happy about. One was a dress-up summer outfit of pink material with short pants. I was embarrassed to wear the outfit and objected so much that I had to wear it only a few times. For cooler weather, she made a long, dark cape that reached almost to the ground. I was very self-conscious when I had to wear this to town.

Sparrow Hunting

There was an abundance of English sparrows around the barnyard. Porter told me that in England, they used to hunt sparrows for food. One night he took me sparrow hunting. We took a lantern and went to the henhouse. There he caught a few sparrows and wrung their necks. Then we removed the feathers and cleaned the sparrows for my mother to cook. They were not especially tasty. One such venture was enough.

Snakes

According to the centennial history of Edgerton, before the land was cleared for planting in an area near Edgerton, there were rattlesnakes, copperheads, and spotted adders, but in 1843, a fire that followed a drought swept through the area and destroyed the snakes. We had few snakes on our farm. My first encounter was when I decided to climb up a straw stack standing in the field. Just as I reached the top, I saw a snake, probably a garter snake, lying there. I lost no time getting away. One day when I was walking along one of the rail fences, I saw a big black snake that crawled away. When we were haying one year, the men killed a black snake that was at least five feet long.

Narrow Escapes

When one of my uncles was working as a hired man for my father, he bought his first car, a used one. It turned out to have a lot of mechanical problems. One day, my uncle invited my mother and me to go to Edgerton in his car. Just as we got onto the railroad tracks that ran through town, the car stalled. A passenger train was coming down the track. We watched the train coming as my uncle tried to get the car started. Finally, with the train still coming, the car started and we got off the track just in time.

One year the threshing machine was in a field reached by going through a gateway at a right angle, with little clearance with a big anchor fencepost. My job was to help on the wagon that took bags of grain from the threshing machine to the granary in the barn. At the barn, the team of horses had to back the wagon up to the entrance. I was in the wagon, pulling the bags of grain to the back of the wagon for the men to carry into the granary. One of the horses, possibly kicking at flies, apparently kicked the other horse and the team took off, with me in the wagon, the reins on the ground. The unguided horses took the wagon through the gate at full speed, fortunately missing the corner post, and ran into the field. My father on the straw stack saw the team coming into the field and realized what was happening. He ran toward the team and grabbed a bridle to slow them down to a stop. That was a narrow escape for me.

Helping Others

Mutual aid, that is, exchange of work for threshing and silo filling, was an accepted practice; the unwritten rules were well recognized by all the participating farmers. Crisis situations brought a different type of action. When a bad windstorm blew down a neighbor's tobacco shed, my father joined other neighbors in picking up pieces of the destroyed building so it could be rebuilt. When fire destroyed the barn on a farm a few miles away, my father took team and wagon, shovel and fork, to join others in cleaning up the debris. There was no thought of being paid to come to the help of others in these kinds of situations.

Gypsies

One summer day, we saw gypsies with their horse-drawn covered wagons driving along the road past our farm. We had never had gypsies before and had not heard that they were in the area. We had no idea why they had chosen to take this road. But they went on their way without stopping near our farm. I knew that gypsies were not welcomed by people in our area.

Funerals

When growing up, I heard the adults talk about deaths and funerals, but this was quite remote. Then, when I was twelve, Mr. Walrath died in the hospital in Janesville. My parents' bedroom was cleared

out so that the casket with his body in it could be placed in the bedroom overnight. The funeral was held the next day in the Walraths'
living room. I had to sit with my parents for the service. Afterward,
a funeral procession to the cemetery in Edgerton took place. The
motor-driven hearse was followed by a mix of cars and horse-driven
buggies. We, in our horse and buggy, must have been near the end; it
seemed as though the procession must have been a half-mile long.

Problem Behavior

I could not help but become aware of problem or deviant behavior
on the part of some individuals I knew by the time I was ten or
twelve years old. For example, a nearby farm family had a teenage girl
staying with them, I think in foster care. The man worked her in the
fields and other types of farm work. One day he was observed, from
a distance, beating her with a heavy leather tug from a harness. No
outsider interfered.

Mrs. Walrath's sister's husband could be abusive when under the
influence of alcohol. On an occasion when the sister had been beaten
badly, she came to stay with Mrs. Walrath. The following Sunday,
when we were all out in the front yard, the husband drove up in his
motorcycle with a sidecar to get his wife back. Mrs. Walrath saw him
coming and came down the path from the house with a stove poker
in her hand, making him leave without his wife.

The middle-aged wife, without children, on a nearby farm began
to have changed behavior patterns. She insisted that the milking and
other chores be done early so that by four o'clock in the afternoon
she and her husband could be ready to go in their car to visit someone.

One day, Mr. Walrath drove by the house and smelled smoke. He went to the house and found that she had put a shovel hot from the stove ashes in a closet and set clothes on fire. She started shouting at her husband, even when others were present. One summer day, my father, the hired man, and I were working in a field and heard her shouting my father's name for help. He went and found both the wife and the husband on the house roof where he had gone for some repair work. A bloodied hammer was lying on the roof. She had hit her husband in the head with it. In the process of the altercation, the ladder had been knocked down. She asked my father to put up the ladder and help her get down off the roof. When he did so, she said, "Thank you."

Law and Order

During my years on the farm, I never saw a sheriff's car or police vehicle in our neighborhood or on the highway that passed the country school. Edgerton had only one police officer as far as I knew. Everyone knew him and knew that his office was next to the small jail. The Town of Fulton had a part-time constable. When a drunken local resident got on the stage and interrupted a program one night at the town hall, he was called to take the drunk away.

Saturday Night Street Entertainment in Edgerton

Once in a while on a summer Saturday night in Edgerton, the activities of outsiders would provide some entertainment. A small Salvation Army band from Janesville would set up on the main street outside one of the stores. They would play their instruments and sing gospel songs. When a small crowd of onlookers gathered to watch, someone from the Salvation Army would ask for contributions.

Of quite a different nature was the diversion offered by other outsiders. A pair of men would set up their huckster operation on a corner on the side of the street opposite the stores. They would hold up a bottle of "medicine" that cured all kinds of ailments and cost only one dollar. They attracted a small crowd of men and boys and made some sales. It is likely that the medicine that cured almost anything was mostly alcohol.

Fragrances and Odors

During the course of a year, a variety of odors and fragrances, repeated year after year, were associated with the farm setting. There were unpleasant odors, notably the smell of the manure at the time the year's accumulation in the barnyard was taken to the fields in midsummer and the unmistakable odor in the nighttime air of a skunk who had sprayed its yellow vile-smelling fluid in defending itself. Then there were the unforgettable fragrances—fruit trees in bloom and newly mowed hay drying in the sun.

Epilogue

Back to the Farm, 1943– 1944

Fourteen years after my last summer on the farm in 1929, I unexpectedly found myself back on the farm as its operator and then as its owner. The event that prompted my return was the death of my father on June 23, 1943, after being kicked in the chest by one of the horses he was hitching to a piece of farm equipment.

I had spent the first six of those fourteen years as a student at the University of Wisconsin in Madison. I earned a bachelor's of science degree in 1932 with a major in agricultural journalism and an equal amount of work in soils, and a master's of science degree in 1933 in agricultural journalism. I was then recruited to be in a graduate program in rural sociology at the university. The last year of the program was at the University of Minnesota. I expected to return to Madison to work on my doctoral dissertation. But my major professor had other plans for me. He had already arranged for me to join the faculty at what is now called the Colorado State University at Fort Collins. This opportunity had opened up after a rapid expansion of federal funds for sociological research into problems associated with the Great Depression. I was in the Department of Economics, Sociology, and History, starting as assistant professor. After three years, in September 1938, I received an unexpected offer to be regional sociologist in a new office being opened in Amarillo, Texas, by the U.S. Department of Agriculture's Bureau of Agricultural Economics. I was to be the leader for the program of the Division of Farm Population and Rural Life. The region included Colorado, Kansas, New Mexico, and parts of Oklahoma and Texas. Late in 1939, I was invited to Washington, D.C., to direct a nationwide study of Farm Security Administration borrowers, research for which funds had already been approved.

After the Japanese attack on Pearl Harbor on December 7, 1941, the nation's efforts were directed at winning the war. Men were called into military service, including some of my acquaintances in the U.S. Department of Agriculture. The programs of the department were all directed toward supporting the war effort, including setting production goals for food and ensuring a supply of labor to produce the food. A nighttime blackout was imposed on the Washington area. Some, including me, were trained to detect poison gas. When the government decided to decentralize some of its activities, I was moved in 1942 to Cincinnati, Ohio, to continue my working association with the Farm Security Administration's national staff, most of whom were moved to Cincinnati. Some of my professional colleagues and friends, about my age, were volunteering for military service. In the spring of 1943, I applied for a commission in the U.S. Navy, through the recruiting office in Cincinnati. I was hoping I would be placed in military government as some of my colleagues in sociology had been.

By this time, I was married and had a two-year-old son. In mid-June, the three of us went to visit my parents on the farm, before I went into service. Soon after our return, a call came saying my father was in the hospital. I immediately went back to Edgerton and found that he had no chance of surviving. This was the first year in all my father's years of farming that he did not have a hired man. A few days after the funeral, my commission came through. I explained the situation to the naval recruiting officer. He recommended that I contribute to the war effort by going back to the farm. In the space of a few days, I had taken leave from my position in the U.S. Department of Agriculture, moved our household goods back to the farm, and put on my overalls and taken up where I had left off fourteen years earlier, except in a different role. Now I was the decision maker.

A neighbor's son had just graduated from high school. His father offered to let him work for me as a monthly hired man. At haying time I persuaded Nick, who so often worked for my father on a standby basis, to help out. When a neighbor saw the corn needed cultivating, he came with his tractor and did the work.

When my father died, the tobacco crop had not yet been planted. My first decision was to not plant the crop; that would cut down on labor requirements. Instead, I put in corn. In the mid-1930s, electricity had finally come to the farm through the Rural Electrification Administration created by the New Deal. Now it would be possible to initiate a major project, putting running water in the house and barn and indoor plumbing in the house. This meant hiring a man to dig a trench for water pipes from the well to the house and from the well across the road to the barn. He also had to dig a trench for the septic tank field, which went toward the orchard area. The installation was done by a hardware dealer in Edgerton, who fortunately had all the needed equipment in stock.

My father had not used the silo for two or three years for some reason. The owner of the silo filler, who had been a country school classmate, helped me get the wooden stave silo in shape to be used that fall. Another decision made in the fall was to keep eight hogs for brood sows rather than the six my father usually had; one reason was to make up part of the income lost by not growing tobacco.

When the estate was settled, I bought out my mother's interest in the farm and took on the balance of the debt my father owed on the loan he had from a government agency, the National Farm Loan Association, when he had purchased the farm. My mother decided to buy a small house, with garden space, in Edgerton and moved her things there.

I decided to buy a tractor. Dealers did not have new ones because of the war. I bought a used tractor, a small one that pulled two plows and had a cultivator and other equipment. I had never driven a tractor and knew nothing about maintaining one. Fortunately, as spring approached, a neighbor helped get the tractor ready to be used. I had no hired help for the spring planting. My wife, who had never lived on a farm before, learned to drive the tractor and did most of the spring plowing. Her mother came to stay with us for a while and look after our young son and help with meals.

There were a few things I had not learned to do when growing up on the farm. One was to castrate the young male pigs and lambs and to dock the lamb tails. A neighbor, my father's age, did this for me without charge. My father had always sheared the sheep with special shears, but I had never tried to do this. I was able to find a farmer who sheared sheep for other people for a fee. He sheared my sheep with his electric clippers.

I decided to use purchased hybrid seed corn rather than the open-pollinated seed corn my father always selected from one year's crop to use the next year. I chose three different hybrids, one an early-maturing variety to get an early crop of corn to feed the hogs. I also wanted to use commercial fertilizer when planting the corn in order to get a bigger yield. My uncle lent me his corn planter, which had an attachment so the fertilizer would drop in the soil correctly. The corn planter was the only piece of equipment on our farm I had never used, but I had no problem with it.

I did not have a hired man in 1944 as I did the previous year. At one point, my uncle had his son, my cousin, come and help for a few days. At haying time, I got Nick to come and help. Just before grain harvest, I had a call from a storekeeper in Edgerton who said two boys were looking for work. I went to see them and hired them on a trial basis. They were high school boys out of Chicago who had never been on a farm. One of the first things I had to tell them was not to smoke around the barn. The shocks of grain they made soon fell down despite my efforts to teach them. The two proved to be of little help, so I took them back to Edgerton and they returned to Chicago.

Being on the farm gave me a firsthand opportunity to see how some of the federal government's wartime activities worked at the local level and to hear my farmer neighbors express their concerns and opinions. For example, at the time of one of the drives to sell war bonds, I was visited by a neighbor who asked if I wanted to buy a war bond. On two or three occasions, a man I did not know stopped by unannounced to talk with me. I knew he was a member of the county Selective Service Board, checking to see if my farming operations justified my being deferred from military service. I went to a meeting of farmers and found myself being asked to explain why the Department of Agriculture's food production program seemed to give preference to pork production over beef production. I had no direct knowledge of the reason for the department's policy on this matter. When I went to the annual meeting of the Township Committee for the Agricultural Adjustment Administration, I was elected alternate member of the committee.

My farmer neighbors supported the war effort without question, but when I was sitting with several of them during a break in threshing activities one day, they questioned how or if the government's big debt to pay for the war would ever be repaid. We finished the work for the last member of the threshing ring (mutual aid group) just before noon in August 1944. After the meal, the owner of the threshing machine put out a washtub of cold soft drinks and beer. All of us sat in the shade in the front yard of the house to relax and talk before heading for home. The talk turned to the purchase of a grain combine by a farmer nearby; this meant that he no longer participated in a mutual aid arrangement to get his grain threshed. There was general agreement that this was the beginning of a trend whereby each farmer would own his own combine or have his work done on a custom basis. It was only a matter of time before there would no longer be groups like our threshing ring.

During my years away from the farm, my country school had been closed; the children were now in a new central school district and transported by bus to Edgerton. The country schoolhouse had been converted into a residence. The high school now had a vocational agriculture department whose teacher had been one of my college classmates. A farmer no longer took his horses to the blacksmith to be shod; the blacksmith came to the farm. After a winter snowstorm, the local farmers no longer cleared the road; the snowplows of a unit of local government did that job. Now nearly all farmers had a tractor; some cut their horses to one team. Milking machines had replaced hand milking to a large extent. New Deal programs had affected agricultural practices on every farm, including soil improvement and soil conservation. Now the wartime program had direct influence, for example, by price controls on the farm products sold and by rationing of gasoline and of some foods.

By early summer of 1944, it was becoming apparent that it was not going to be realistic for my family to continue to live on and operate the farm indefinitely. When the selection committee for the Rock County Shorthorn Breeders Association chose two of my cows for sale, I agreed to have them included. I was pleased when one of my cows, with her calf, brought the highest price of any animal in the sale, bringing more than the animals of better-known breeders. I advertised in the Shorthorn Breeders publication that the herd was for sale. One day the representative of the county association brought a Chicago businessman to the farm. He bought the entire herd, except for the bull, and when he took delivery he paid in cash.

I did not want to sell the farm so I inquired of a farm management company about its taking on the management function. I was told the 120-acre farm was too small to be of interest. I did not want to be an absentee landlord; this would be counter to my values. So I reluctantly put the farm up for sale. It sold quickly to a local businessman, who planned to have a renter. The next step was to have an auction to dispose of all the remaining livestock, equipment, and the grain, hay, and corn standing in the field. I contracted with the best auctioneer I knew, and he handled all the details of advertising and collecting money from the buyers.

Although I had been on leave from my position with the Department of Agriculture, I had kept contact. Two members of the division's staff stopped at the farm to visit me, one overnight. When I could get away, I made quick trips back to Cincinnati a couple of times to check on the work being done on my research by the professional staff member who was continuing in my absence. Once I was called into the Washington office to take part in the planning stage of what was to be a major national research project. I was free to return to my job at my discretion.

With the farm sold and the auction held, my wife and son left to visit her sister, then living in Arizona. I put most of our household goods in storage in Janesville. What we needed for temporary use went on the two-wheeled trailer made by one of my uncles in 1926 and in the Ford Model A my father had left. When the house was cleaned out, on October 24, I turned the house key over to the new owner. I reluctantly said good-bye to the farm and headed back to Cincinnati to take up as a rural sociologist where I had left off sixteen months earlier.

I have been asked what the effect was on my life of growing up on a farm. First of all, it affected my college plans. At the time, I thought I wanted to be a farmer, so the only type of college I seriously considered was an agricultural one. I went to the College of Agriculture at the University of Wisconsin.

Without the farm background, I probably would not have tried out for and made the college's livestock and dairy cattle judging teams. My participation in these teams took me to Chicago, Kansas City, and Waterloo, Iowa, when my team competed with teams from other colleges from all across the United States.

Although I never got to farm as a lifetime career, the farming background did influence my professional career. I was never interested in a position that was not somehow farm or rural related. Thus, my professional career was in the U.S. Department of Agriculture as a rural sociologist and at Cornell University as a rural sociologist. In some ways, my work and my teaching benefited from my farm background, for instance, my research on low-income farmers and my community studies.

In a more general sense, I am sure that my continuing interest in farm and rural policy and in changes in agricultural technology and the structure of agriculture were influenced by my farm background.

Another effect was that I never lost my interest in gardening. When we went to Cornell in 1946, I insisted that we have a place with enough land for a garden and fruit. For years, we grew food for fresh use, freezing, and canning. During the years I had a garden, every January I welcomed the seed and nursery catalogs that came in the mail. I went through them, page by page, to find items I might want to order and plant that season.

Perhaps an indication of the lifelong influence of my farm rearing was the astute observation of my then-twelve-year-old son at lunch one day: "Dad, anyone can tell that you are a boy from the country."

Suggested Readings

Apps, Jerry. *Barns of Wisconsin.* 3rd ed. Madison: Wisconsin Historical Society Press, 2010.

——. *Cheese: The Making of a Wisconsin Tradition.* Amherst, WI: Amherst Press, 1998.

——. *Every Farm Tells a Story.* Minneapolis, MN: Voyageur Press, 2005.

——. *Living a Country Year.* Minneapolis, MN: Voyageur Press, 2007.

——. *Old Farm: A History.* Madison: Wisconsin Historical Society Press, 2008.

——. *One-Room Country School.* Amherst, WI: Amherst Press, 1996.

——. *The People Came First: A History of Wisconsin Cooperative Extension.* Madison: University of Wisconsin–Extension, 2002.

Buenker, John D. *The History of Wisconsin.* Vol. 4, *The Progressive Era, 1893–1914.* Madison: Wisconsin Historical Society Press, 1998.

The Edgerton Story: A History of Edgerton, Wisconsin. Edgerton: Edgerton Centennial, Inc., 1953.

Glad, Paul. *The History of Wisconsin.* Vol. 5, *War, a New Era, and Depression, 1914–1940.* Madison: Wisconsin Historical Society Press, 1990.

Prairie Farmer's Reliable Directory of Farmers and Breeders, Rock County, Wisconsin. Chicago: Prairie Farmer, 1919.

Schafer, Joseph. *A History of Agriculture in Wisconsin.* Madison: Wisconsin Historical Society Press, 1922.